OUTWARD BOUND
SAILING HANDBOOK

TROWBRIDGE COLLEGE

AUTHOR: BALCOMBE, Martin

TITLE   Outward Bound Sailing Handbook

No.

D0238412

'ST BE RETURN

Also available

OUTWARD BOUND
SAILING HANDBOOK

Martin Balcombe

WARD LOCK

I would like to thank
Annie Jukes and Dorothy McPhee

A WARD LOCK BOOK
First published in the UK in 1995
by Ward Lock
Wellington House
125 Strand
London WC2R 0BB

A Cassell Imprint

Distributed in Australia by
Capricorn Link (Australia) Pty Ltd
2/13 Carrington Road, Castle Hill, NSW 2154

British Library Cataloguing-in-Publication data
A catalogue record for this book is available from the British Library

ISBN 0–7063–7361–8

Front cover photograph: Stephen Whitehorne
Back cover photograph: Mark Allen Publishing
Illustrations: Tim Scrivener
Typesetting and design: Ben Cracknell
Printed and bound in Finland by Werner Söderström Oy

Contents

About Outward Bound®

The Outward Bound Trust provides high-quality courses in a range of exciting outdoor activities. Our fully qualified instructors maintain the highest standards of tuition, and our safety record is second to none. Everyone who takes an Outward Bound course enjoys a rewarding and memorable experience, the benefits of which will last a lifetime.

Outward Bound courses have been available in Britain since 1941. The original courses were the outcome of a meeting between Kurt Hahn, the educator, with Lawrence Holt, the owner of a shipping line. The marriage of the worlds of education and business is a vital feature of the Outward Bound movement. The courses are both a valuable adjunct to formal education and an important part of career development.

From its beginnings in Britain the Outward Bound movement has spread throughout the world, with 38 centres in 23 countries.

A typical course in the UK lasts from one to three weeks and may be based at one of our five national centres or take the form of an expeditionary journey by foot or by sailing boat in a wilderness setting. We run courses for all age groups, from 14 to 70!

The Outward Bound Trust also designs programmes to help companies through periods of change. This may involve developing leadership skills for young managers or assisting in building cohesive teams. The courses balance challenging outdoor tasks with reflection and review. They are specially designed so participants can translate what they gain back to their working environment.

After an Outward Bound experience, people discover many positive attributes about themselves. They become more confident; they learn to share; to lead and to follow; to understand their own strengths and to work together as a group. By safeguarding each other, they form bonds of trust. They discover that many problems can be solved only with the co-operation of all members of a group.

To find out more about Outward Bound courses or to request a brochure, please contact us at: Outward Bound Trust, PO Box 1219, Windsor, Berkshire SL4 LXR. Tel (01753) 731005

Michael Hobbs
Outward Bound Trust

1

Introduction

Out of the mist the mountains rose magnificently, reaching up their jagged fingertips towards the now blue sky. Our mood of intense concentration was lifted as the sun broke through, bathing the scenery in its warming glow. This break in the weather brought to a close the most difficult part of the passage and Spylgarn *picked up her heels, as if sensing the lightened mood of her two crew. It was a delightful culmination of a challenging and difficult day; the sunshine and fair wind had been earned by our earlier escapades in poor visibility.*

Later, lying to anchor in the little boat with the boom tent snugged down and the stove bubbling away I felt a contented satisfaction that all was well with life. The rewards of sailing are keenly felt and never more so than in a small open boat in beautiful surroundings.

There are many reasons why sailing is such a popular pastime. For some, sailing means an exciting summer's evening with the thrill of racing in close proximity to similar craft, pitting their wits against their competitors to gain the most out of their boats. Others enjoy longer offshore passages, sailing for days or even weeks, enjoying the life of the sea and watching its infinite and changing moods roll by until the passage is completed and harbour reached. Then there are the joys of pottering. The summer weekends 'messing about in boats', getting away from it all into the timeless, relaxing world afloat.

I have enjoyed many different aspects of sailing over the years and have introduced people to the joys of being afloat on diverse boats from dinghies to Outward Bound cutters and from yachts to larger traditional sailing craft. The techniques of sailing are not easily self-taught and usually the best way of getting started is to have a go in other people's boats first. From here the beginner must decide what type of sailing he or she is interested in. It is possible to learn to sail, as I did, on a Brixham trawler. Indeed some people would rather crew on a larger boat, learning how to handle sails, pull the right ropes, take a spell on the helm and enjoy the camaraderie of working well within a team of people rather than cope with the demands of skippering.

Having instructed for a number of years I know that one of the most satisfying times for the trainee is the first time thay are really in charge of the boat. This does not happen fully until the instructor, owner or more experienced person gets off the boat. At Outward Bound we talk about 'consequential learning'. We see that people learn, understand and remember more when practical work has real consequences. With the instructor at a greater distance the mind is focussed wonderfully and the thrill of realizing that you can put into practice what you have learned soon takes over.

On the seventh day of a 'Viking Wayfarer' course the crews of the two boats were working well and were aiming to complete a full day's passage without an instructor on board. From here to the end of the Outward Bound expedition the responsibilities would increase each day. That night they would need to plan the whole of the three day return journey, checking the forecast, the tides, the charts and the pilot books. It seemed a lot to expect of them but they had been building up to it for a week now.

They had practised anchoring with the instructors on board and now they had to do it for real! As Morven Cameron *tacked her way in, the safety boat stood in a little closer. The skipper was looking a bit nervous but kept the boat sailing well as they approached a suitable depth and as she slowed the cutter down I knew it was a good job. 'Let go the anchor' came a little too quietly for the crew in the bow with the staysail flapping around his ears. When the chain eventually rattled over the bow roller they were a little deeper than they might have chosen to be but the skipper was looking much more relaxed as the sails came down.*

On Fiona MacLean *things were not running quite as smoothly as they had just missed a tack. They got around on the second attempt and were discussing how to make the final approach. The anchorage looked smaller with the other cutter sitting there and manouevring room was tight. Mike, their skipper was under peer pressure to sail on in like the others. He had had quite a challenging day and felt under pressure to do well. He was getting used to taking command and it was pleasing to see him take a strong decision. As they sailed up astern of* Morven, *the staysail came down and four oars appeared in their crutches. They pulled their way up into the gentle breeze and dropped the anchor neatly in a good spot.*

I was pleased with both crews: they had sailed reasonably well but above all kept the boats safe and operated within their abilities. They had learned when to discuss a problem and when to respond quickly to the skipper's decision. Their seamanship was developing and they were learning fast.

Many people have gained their first experience of sailing during an Outward Bound course. They may have had a day sail on one of the traditionally rigged 9m (28ft) open cutters, or some sessions in one of the smaller dinghies. The passage above describes one of our sailing expedition courses where people come for one or two weeks and learn to sail the cutters. There are many other ways in which people start sailing and it is one of the joys of the sport that there is such a variety of activity available on all shapes and sizes of boats.

Most would agree that the techniques of sailing are best mastered in a small and simple boat. Generally speaking, the smaller the boat the sooner you are likely to be able to take charge of it yourself. Another advantage of a small boat is that it will forgive mistakes less easily so you can learn from them quicker! If you get things wrong you might get wet of course, but that is all part of the fun.

For these reasons this book concentrates on dinghy sailing as an introduction to the sport. It is intended as a guide for those wishing to learn to sail and aims to advise the beginner on everything from how to go about getting involved to how to learn sailing techniques and manoeuvres. Everything you learn will be useful on other boats and the basic awareness of the wind direction and the understanding of how to harness it can be applied across the board. The book cannot replace practical learning and experience of course but it should prove a useful companion for the novice, providing a reminder of lessons learned and help steer the improving sailor towards better techniques.

I have inevitably used many technical terms in the book but have attempted to explain them when they are first used. Words found in the glossary are in italics the first time they appear.

Note: Words and phrases such as 'helmsman' and 'man overboard' are used throughout this book to refer to both men and women. These words are in common usage and are not intended to discriminate in any way.

2

First steps

Sailing is a much easier sport to participate in than people often imagine. It is not necessary to have your own boat in order to enjoy it and indeed it would be wiser to see how you enjoy sailing before investing in one. After having a go in different boats owned by others, by a club, or sailing school you will be in a better position to decide what sort of craft best suits you.

Most people involved in sailing will aspire to owning their own boat eventually and as long as something simple is required it can be supported by the most modest of incomes. Be warned however that by buying this book you are clearly interested in launching yourself into a highly addictive pastime that most of us involved in will freely admit has a habit of happily entertaining you for vast amounts of time and swallowing as much money as you care to put into it! We light-heartedly complain about the cost of bits and bobs bought for the boat but happily lavish care, money and attention on our pride and joy nonetheless. If you do end up buying your own dinghy then some simple ground rules are needed to keep costs down.

Keeping the costs down:

- Keep your desires modest and enjoy the simple pleasures of being afloat.
- Do not buy one until you know what you are looking at or you can take someone who does.
- Be more ready to compromise on your choice of boat than on your upper budget level.
- Take a practical approach to maintaining your boat and keeping it in good condition.
- Beware of letting your enthusiasm get carried away when using your credit card in a chandler's shop. There is usually a great temptation to buy much more than you really need!

It may be that you have pots of money and are tempted by a shiny model and the salesperson's patter at a boat show. If you do get your own boat think early about insurance. This should cover possible damage when towing, theft (check any restrictions here as to whether it should be locked 'immobilized' etc.) and third party to cover damage to other vessels and property. This latter section is a requirement in order to sail with many clubs.

I would still advise to go and try other people's boats first, so let us consider how you go about doing that.

Sailing clubs

Most countries have a national association or governing body which will advise you on the whereabouts of affiliated sailing clubs in your area. The *Royal Yachting Association (RYA)* is the national governing body for sailing and boating in the UK (see appendix 1 for the contact details of governing bodies in other countries). They will probably ask you what you have done before and what sort of sailing you are interested in so that they can put you on to a club that can meet your needs. Alternatively you may find details of club activity in your local leisure or sports centre or library. Most sailing clubs are keen to welcome beginners and may organize special courses or weekends for novices. They will have a programme of activities through the weekday evenings with weekend sailing as well. Their racing programme will be for various classes of boat and individual clubs will have different classes that they favour.

If you are fortunate enough to have more than one club in your area then a bit of research will help you decide which to join. Obviously the classes of boat sailed will be an important factor so go down and watch and see what appeals. Much more important at this stage however will be the provision the club makes for beginners and how welcome you are made to feel. A small number of clubs seem to have a very stiff approach and you feel extremely conspicuous and out of place as soon as you walk in. Do not give up straight away, you may have just picked a bad time, but if they really have not got anything organized for beginners then this is not the place for you.

The other factors to consider might be how easy it is for you to travel there, whether they have any club boats that members can use, and how easy it is to get to crew on other people's boats if you do not intend to get your own. I recommend that as a beginner, you go to a club which in addition to being affiliated is also accredited as a teaching establishment in the same way as a sailing school (see page 12). You can then expect them to offer a structured programme for beginners and provide quality instruction with safe equipment. These courses would also then lead towards a nationally recognized certificate (see below). Club courses are often run over a series of weekends and have the advantage (over a sailing school course) of helping you get to know other people at your local club as well as getting you started with other like-minded and not so competent souls!

For those who do not have a sailing club of some sort really close then the job is a little harder but there are a huge number of different types of water to sail on from estuaries on the coast to inland rivers, reservoirs and even gravel pits. You may find somewhere closer than you expect. Many people who enjoy sailing live a little distance from the nearest stretch of suitable water but are keen enough to make the journey regularly to pursue their sport.

Sailing school courses and national certificates

You could start by going away and attending a course at one of the accredited sailing schools. This would be a good way to learn the basics if your local club does not run courses, or if you cannot attend those that they do run, or if perhaps you would just rather go away on a course. A great deal can be learnt in a short time and it can prove a fun way to learn to sail while enjoying a holiday and meeting new people. In the UK the RYA administers a series of schemes which cover every aspect of 'yachting' from windsurfing to power-boating and from dinghy sailing to ocean cruising.

The RYA dinghy scheme gives a progression of certificates from level one 'Start Sailing', to level five 'Advanced Skills'. Most schools offer a five-day combination course covering level one and the level two, 'Basic Skills' syllabus. This will provide a good introduction to dinghy sailing and by the end of the course students should be competent to take out a dinghy without an instructor in light winds. They should have a fair awareness of safety and a basic understanding of the sailing process. The great advantage of attending a structured course is that it gives a record of your progress and sets specific goals for achievement. If you then wish to continue your learning with a further course at a later stage, you will have a better idea of which course to book and the instructor will be able to pitch the teaching at your level. RYA sailing schools are listed in the booklet *Dinghy Sailing and Keelboat Courses*, which is updated annually and available from the RYA. The keelboat scheme follows a similar progression through levels one to four but covers the skills for boats larger than dinghies, filling the gap between dinghies and cruising yachts.

For the availability of courses in other countries contact the governing body who should be able to help (see Appendix 1).

Personal equipment

Once you have decided how you will first be going sailing you can then consider what equipment you need to get started. This could get extremely expensive if you allow it to but it need not at this stage.

The dedicated 'gear freak' will march into the biggest outdoor gear store or chandlery and buy up everything they could possibly need for a whole season of hard sailing. Standing next to them, a lesser mortal with the usual end-of-the-month overdraft might feel that sailing is reserved for those with pots of money who can splash out huge amounts. This really is not the case. Your fellow beginner may be much more comfortable in a drysuit but if comfort is what you are after then a glass of wine in front of the fire watching television has a lot to be said for it! I mention the drysuit as it is one of the most expensive pieces of personal equipment you could buy, not because I doubt their comfort and value. My drysuit is very comfortable but I did manage to sail without one for ten years without getting hypothermia so they are by no means essential!

Essential equipment

If you are heading off on an organized course they should let you know what you will need to take and what is supplied. If sailing at a club then it may be possible to borrow a *buoyancy aid* at least. At first you should aim to make do with things you have anyway and buy as little as possible; after all, you may not take to sailing!

Footwear

A pair of light-weight training shoes that you do not mind getting wet are usually the best option.

Inner layers

Generally avoid cotton where possible. It is likely that you will get at least a bit damp and cotton tends to stay damp and feel cold. You might be more comfortable in a swimming costume than underpants. Tracksuit bottoms are better if made from artificial fabric rather than the cotton 'jogger' type. In warmer weather long johns, leggings or even shorts might do. On the top half, again avoid cottons if you have the option. I have a few long sleeve 'thermal' shirts which seem to be universally useful across a range of activities.

Mid layer

It is impossible to advise exactly how much to wear as what you need will depend entirely on the weather, how long you will be out for, the type of boat you are sailing (some are much more energetic than others) and your own ability to retain body heat. Modern fleece tops are much warmer than cotton sweatshirts. Take one with your kit so you have something warm to put on if you need it. Woollen jumpers can be as warm but tend to soak up more water and take longer to dry out.

Waterproofs

A windproof and preferably waterproof jacket or *cagoule* will be needed on all but the warmest of days. Ideally it should be not too long, medium weight and have tight closing wrist and neck seals. You may have something which will do for starting out; what do you normally use when it rains? As long as it is not an umbrella it may do the job! Waterproof trousers are often useful too, if only to keep the wind off.

Buoyancy aid

It is important to wear some means of additional flotation while in small boats and a buoyancy aid is generally accepted as the most appropriate for use in dinghies. It is basically a waistcoat of padded foam, usually secured by a zip and a waist belt. It should fit over your sailing clothing, be quite snug without being too tight and it should not ride up over your head in active use. A whistle is a sensible addition for use in emergencies. Buoyancy devices are classified as buoyancy aids or life-jackets according to the amount of buoyancy – measured in newtons – they provide. To classify as a life-jacket, the device should have at least 150 newtons (15kg/33lb) of buoyancy. Buoyancy aids usually have 50 or 100 newtons (5kg/11lb or 10.5kg/23lb) of buoyancy.

A fully inflated 150 newton life-jacket will keep a person afloat and the right way up even if unconscious. There are two types: those with and those without integral foam in addition to the inflatable section on the front. The type with integral buoyancy tends to be bulky and can be an encumbrance when you are in a dinghy and need to be able to move about freely. When in the water, the bulk of the foam also tends to get in the way when you are trying to swim around the dinghy untangling

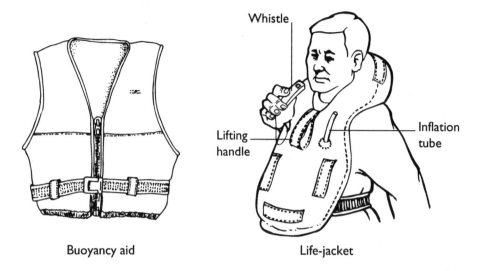

| Buoyancy aid | Life-jacket |

2.1 Buoyancy aid and life-jacket.

sheets and organizing the righting. Although less bulky, the type without integral buoyancy is not suited to use for dinghy sailing. It is very bulky when inflated and of no use for short periods in the water.

A 100 newton buoyancy aid does not have enough buoyancy to keep an unconscious wearer afloat the right way up but it does give more support than a 50 newton device, which is only designed to help you stay afloat. Nevertheless, for inshore dinghy sailing where a safety boat is on the water, the most suitable first choice is probably a 50 newton buoyancy aid, which is comfortable to wear and not too bulky. See figure 2.1.

Hat
Most body heat is lost through the head, therefore a woolly hat or balaclava does a great deal to keep you warm in cooler conditions.

Crash helmet
This may sound extreme but many courses for beginners offer these as standard, particularly for children. They cannot really be described as essential but their use by any beginner should be considered, as a crack across the head by the *boom* can be very serious. Watersports helmets should fit well and offer protection to the vulnerable areas of forehead and temples.

Spares

Do not forget a towel and a full set of warm clothes to change into when you get out.

Upgrading your equipment

This is where you have to start weighing up the priorities. The more sailing you do the better value decent kit becomes and the more occasion you will have to be glad you bought it. I offer the following list on a purely subjective basis that assumes you have something that does the job in each of the essential areas as listed above. The order of priority is my own but is based on the assumption that you are sailing a dinghy in which getting wet every now and then is part of the learning process.

Waterproofs

Where this appears on your priority list depends on whether you have been able to make do with items you had already and how effective they have been. There is no doubt that a decent set of waterproofs can make a huge difference to your comfort and it is usually worth investing in something appropriate. The one-piece suit is excellent for dinghy sailing and is usually fairly light weight and comfortable to wear. If you intend to sail larger boats then a separate set of jacket and trousers may be more versatile. A jacket is generally more expensive than a smock but is easier to get on and a bit more versatile. For dinghy sailing you will not want it too long or heavy as that would feel restrictive. *Salopettes* are less likely to start coming down in active use as trousers with an elastic waist tend to. This usually happens at a crucial moment when you want to be at your nimblest such as dropping the spinnaker, or pulling the trolley up the slip at the end of the day with an increasingly eccentric walk on full display to onlookers!

Wetsuit

Sailing in wet clothes can get cold and uncomfortable so a wetsuit can ease this problem on the not-so-sunny days. It will also allow you to enjoy sailing in a greater range of weather conditions. A wetsuit does not keep you dry but works by trapping a layer of water between your body and the suit. Your body heats this up and the wetsuit prevents this warm water from escaping and circulating cooler water around your body. Wetsuits come in different weights of neoprene and different styles according to what would best suit your purpose. A *longjohn* covers not just your legs but comes up to your chest and over your shoulders. The arms are not covered but this allows more freedom of movement and you are less likely to overheat when working hard. A longjohn is an extremely versatile piece of equipment which can be used for a variety of activities, particularly when you want to be able to move freely and do not expect to be fully immersed frequently or for long periods. It can be worn with a T-shirt and fleece underneath if necessary and with a decent cagoule over the top I find I am warm enough in most dinghy sailing conditions. It can be added to with a wetsuit jacket or *bolero* top which provides considerable extra warmth but does tend to restrict movement somewhat. The *steamer* or one-piece suit is useful for activities where you expect to be in the water more frequently but is less versatile than the longjohn and bolero. Whatever wetsuit you choose be sure to select one that fits snugly as too much room inside will make you cold (due to too much circulation of water) and uncomfortable.

Footwear
Wetsuit socks are shaped from neoprene and help avoid that soggy feeling that goes with having wet feet for a while. They have no sole and must be worn inside your wet training shoes or perhaps with a pair of plastic beach shoes. Wetsuit boots have a sole on them so can be worn on their own. Both the above are more suitable than Wellington boots for sailing dinghies as you will often be beach launching and needing to stand in water deeper than wellies. Wellies can also encumber you in the water so the use of them is best kept for sailing larger boats, keelboats and (when you are sure you will not be capsizing) dinghies kept on moorings. A good alternative to these are dinghy boots, which are short, snug, laced boots which cannot fill up with a large amount of water.

Gloves
A suitable pair of gloves not only keeps the hands warm but helps protect them from the rigours of rope handling. They should be tight fitting with a good grip and wear-resistant palms. Full-fingered ones are the warmest whilst those with cut away fingers allow for easier rope handling.

Drysuit
This is a fully waterproof suit, either in one piece or sealed at the waist, with tight closing seals at wrists and neck. Some have ankle seals, others enclose the feet as well. With a drysuit you can vary the amount of

clothing you wear underneath to achieve a comfortable temperature. They must be looked after carefully by rinsing in fresh water after use and dusting with talcum powder after a thorough drying.

Knife

Once you decide that sailing is for you then you should equip yourself with a stainless steel sailing knife. These have a key for undoing *shackles* and a sharp blade. Ropes surround the sailor and on occasions it is important to be able to cut one free.

3

Armchair learning

The purpose of this chapter is to provide the newcomer to sailing with some information to digest before embarking on their first practical session. You will feel that much more prepared and have a little less to learn on the day if you can become familiar with the parts of the boat and what they are called and have begun to understand how the wind works in your favour. Do not get too bogged down with this if you find it difficult to learn this way, after all, learning is best done practically so you will remember things better when you actually see them. You could then use this chapter as a source of reference later on.

Sailors are sometimes criticized for using a bewildering array of technical terminology which can leave the beginner confused and alienated. This is because some people's first experience of crewing a sailing boat is spoiled by being shouted at in what sounds like a totally foreign language by a nervous or manic skipper betraying their own fear or lack of confidence.

Try not to feel put off by the amount of new information. The terminology is not there to make things harder for the beginner. It is simply a way of being precise about pieces of equipment or ropes on the boat. The *jib halyard* is much more simply described as such than 'the white rope with blue flecks in it on the *port* (left hand) side of the *mast* which raises the *jib* sail which is the one in the *bow* (front of the boat)'. As a beginner you will learn much faster if you sail with someone who stays calm when you get things wrong and introduces the essential terminology gradually and with explanations. If you are attending an organized course then you should expect no less but in a less formal arrangement you may have to keep a check on your progress by asking yourself what you have learned each session and writing it down. If you are confused at any time then ask. Anyone taking a beginner sailing must be prepared to think things out well enough in advance to make the time to explain things as you go along.

Figures 3.1 and 3.2 show the majority of terms in common use describing the parts of two typical dinghies.

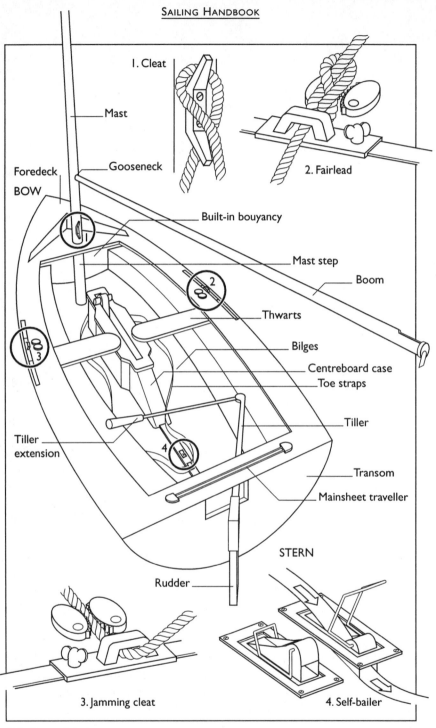

1. Cleat

Mast

Gooseneck

2. Fairlead

Foredeck
BOW

Built-in bouyancy

Mast step

Boom

Thwarts

Bilges

Centreboard case

Toe straps

Tiller

Tiller
extension

Transom

Mainsheet traveller

STERN

Rudder

3. Jamming cleat

4. Self-bailer

3.1 Parts of the boat.

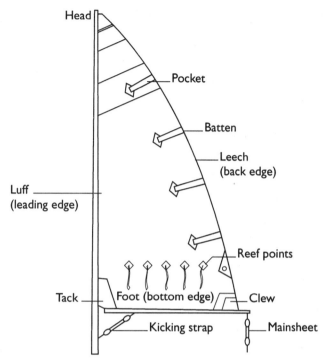

Head

Pocket

Batten

Leech
(back edge)

Luff
(leading edge)

Reef points

Tack

Foot (bottom edge)

Clew

Kicking strap

Mainsheet

3.2 Parts of the sail.

Judging wind strength and direction

There are a number of different forces at work when a sailing boat is making progress under sail and it will help you to make best use of the power of the wind if you have an idea as to why the boat can sail as it does. The first thing is to teach yourself to become aware of the wind. This is a crucial skill for the sailor who will need a closer awareness of the wind and weather than those for whom changes in weather have little significance. Personally, I take great delight in leading a life which is affected by the changes in the natural world around me. In modern-day life in the town it is quite easy to go about your daily round with little regard for changes in wind and weather save a bit of thought on what to wear when looking out of the window in the morning. These same changes can make enormous and dramatic differences to those at sea or working outdoors who have to re-assess their plans constantly in order to work with the natural elements. Sometimes this is particularly unpleasant of course and I would be the first to admit that I do not look forward to the next time I get caught out in a gale at sea or have to retreat off a mountain in foul weather. I accept those times though and they make the times of stunning beauty and perfect conditions all that much more worth striving for. As a beginner at sailing it may be that the need for an awareness of these things is new to you but it is a skill worth developing.

You can begin to work on your wind awareness right away without needing a boat to practise on. It may seem an obvious question to ask but I am often surprised when I ask students where the wind is coming from, at the amount of thought necessary to come up with an answer and at the variety of responses I receive. Start by looking to see if you can spot any visual signs which give you information about the wind. If you can see trees then are the leaves fluttering, the branches moving, or even the whole tree swaying about? These give a visual indication of the strength of the wind even if you are indoors and unable to feel it on your face. Other visual signs can give an indication of wind direction as well as strength. Look to see whether the clouds are visibly moving and if so in which direction. These can show something of a different direction than the wind down at sea level but can help you build up a picture of what might be happening down on the water. Smoke is one of the best visual indicators, giving a good idea of both wind strength and direction. If you are near the water then the waves show you more about the wind. The table on page 34 compares the sea state to wind strength. Look for the direction that moored boats are pointing in as well. They will be pointing head to wind as long as they are not in a tideway but even then there may be *burgees* or flags on them which can give you a clue.

The last but most important way of judging wind direction once you are on board a boat is by feeling it. Again you can get used to this whenever you go outside but feeling the wind on your face is the most versatile method. It is usually obvious to most people whether the wind is coming from roughly ahead or behind them, but when sailing you need to be much more accurate than that. For this you need to keep your head bare at first, particularly your ears. Turn your head until the wind is blowing on your face and listen to the sound of the wind in your ears. As you rotate your head you will hear the wind in one ear or the other or in both. When you hear an equal force on both ears then you are exactly facing the wind direction. This may sound obvious to some but for many it is something that needs a bit of practice to be able to do as quickly as you need to when sailing.

Harnessing the wind
Hull shape

How can a boat use the wind to make progress in any direction? A basic understanding of this will help so we will start with the simplest case – getting blown downwind. If you were to place a plastic lunch box on a pond it would travel in the direction of the wind with no control over its direction. Hardly any of the lunch box is in the water so it offers little resistance and gets blown down quite quickly. Before we discuss sail power we must look at the difference between the lunch box and the *hull* of a boat. The hull is not just designed to sit on top of the water but to travel forwards as well, either pushing the water aside as it goes through it (*displacing*), or lifting itself on top of the water and skimming along (*planing*). Most modern dinghies are designed to *plane* when on a fast point of sailing and so have quite flat sections under the water towards the back of the boat (*aft*). Sailing boats have a bow that is designed to cut through the waves and a smooth hull to offer minimal resistance to forward movement.

In order to steer sailing boats also have a *rudder*, a shaped board which fits on the *transom* and hangs down into the water. It forms the principal means of steering the boat, is controlled by a *tiller* and *tiller extension* and can be raised when in shallow water. If our lunch box were fitted with a rudder then the direction in which it pointed could be adjusted. It would still have a tendency to be blown downwind however as there would be very little of the box in the water resisting this sideways drift. This illustrates an important concept in sailing – the fact that while the boat may be pointing one way, it may well be travelling in a different direction. This difference is called *leeway* (see figure 3.3).

So whilst the hull of a sailing boat offers little resistance to forward movement it also needs to reduce the tendency to drift sideways as our lunch box would do. This is achieved by a combination of the hull shape and either a *keel* or *centreboard*. This sits below the hull and helps prevent the boat drifting sideways through the water a bit like a hot knife cutting through butter. Dinghies have either a centreboard, which is pivoted and swings up into a case to be retracted, or a *daggerboard* which slides up and down in a slot or case.

Going downwind

Going back to our lunch box floating across the pond we can see that the dinghy has several advantages that will help it work more effectively. It has a hull shape that is designed to allow it to travel forwards easily and resist sideways movement, and a rudder to help control its direction. In addition to this it also has sails of course. For a trip downwind across the pond the shape of the sails is relatively unimportant and it is purely the area of the sail and the direct wind pressure on it that provides the force to drive the boat. This force is transmitted from the sail to the hull by the mast and the *rigging*. The sail is adjusted to lie across the boat and the rudder allows us to steer; thus we can make progress downwind in the simplest of manners. This is pretty much how boats were first sailed. They would have been paddled when required to travel up or across the wind and only sailed when the traveller was lucky enough to have the wind roughly behind them.

Sailing across the wind (reaching)

Once we wish to turn the boat in a direction across the wind then the forces involved become a little more complicated and we must abandon the lunch box idea and look to simple aerodynamics for some explanation. When a boat sails at about 90 degrees across the wind direction (called sailing on a *beam reach*) the combination of forces begins to act most effectively. Here the force acting on the sail is no longer purely pushing and aerodynamics play an important part in the generation of sail forces.

As the wind strikes the sail it is deflected to follow the shape of the sail. It gets 'squashed' on the *windward* side (an increase of pressure) and on the *leeward* side it expands to fill the space behind (causing a decrease in pressure on that side). This pressure difference creates an *aerodynamic force* which works to drive the boat along.

Figure 3.4 shows air being deflected smoothly over the surface of the sail. This smooth (*laminar*) airflow is important to ensure that aerodynamic force is most effectively produced. It is therefore important that the sail is presented to the wind at the correct angle otherwise the airflow is turbulent and aerodynamic force is lessened. The angle that the sail presents to the wind can be changed by turning the whole boat or by just adjusting the sail angle (*sail trim*).

The total force produced by the sails acts in a direction about 90 degrees to the angle of the sail and wants to propel the boat sideways as well as forwards. In figure 3.5 the wind arrow is at a suitable angle to the sail for the airflow to be laminar. Imagine you are sitting on a sailing boat facing exactly the same direction as the boat is pointing. Now work through the captions, rotating the book (and therefore the wind

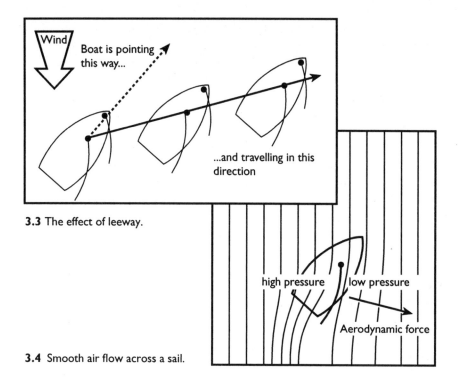

3.3 The effect of leeway.

3.4 Smooth air flow across a sail.

direction) to see roughly how the sails are trimmed and where the aerodynamic force is directed.

Figure 3.5 makes rather large generalizations but I hope it helps. Bear in mind that the wind indicated is the wind direction as it appears to cross the boat (apparent wind). This is affected greatly by your speed (see page 27).

Fortunately the boat does not travel in the direction of the aerodynamic force arrow. As we saw, the sideways element was only moderate when sailing across the wind and is counteracted by the water resistance on the hull, the rudder and the centreboard.

Sailing upwind

A sailing boat cannot sail directly into the wind so there is an optimum angle at which it can work. Imagine a boat pointing directly into the wind. The sails will be flapping freely like a flag, producing no aerodynamic force and therefore no drive. We call this stalled position being

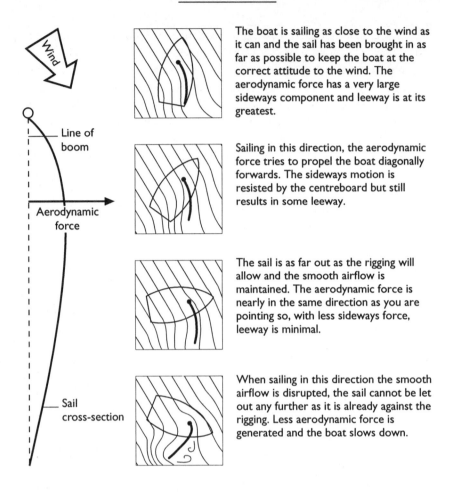

The boat is sailing as close to the wind as it can and the sail has been brought in as far as possible to keep the boat at the correct attitude to the wind. The aerodynamic force has a very large sideways component and leeway is at its greatest.

Sailing in this direction, the aerodynamic force tries to propel the boat diagonally forwards. The sideways motion is resisted by the centreboard but still results in some leeway.

The sail is as far out as the rigging will allow and the smooth airflow is maintained. The aerodynamic force is nearly in the same direction as you are pointing so, with less sideways force, leeway is minimal.

When sailing in this direction the smooth airflow is disrupted, the sail cannot be let out any further as it is already against the rigging. Less aerodynamic force is generated and the boat slows down.

3.5 Direction of aerodynamic force on different points of sailing.

in irons. The boat must be turned away from the wind before the sails will fill with wind and begin to produce forward drive.

As we saw in figure 3.5, the sideways force is most pronounced when the boat sails closest to the wind. The centreboard is needed most and therefore lowered most when the boat is on this *close-hauled* point of sailing. The resistance offered by the centreboard works best when the boat is moving well through the water, so maintaining good boat-speed helps to reduce leeway.

A result of the water resistance from hull, centreboard and rudder is that the dinghy now also begins to *heel* or tip over to leeward. This in its turn is counteracted by the crew shifting their weight more to windward. The boat sails most efficiently when it is fairly level and the centreboard works less efficiently when the boat is heeled, so this use of crew weight to balance the boat is important. See figure 3.6.

A boat sailing close hauled will be sailing slower than one on a *reach*. This is partly due to the forward drive being reduced and partly because of the greater tendency for the boat to heel on this point of sailing. When it is heeled over the boat will move through the water less efficiently and will be less likely to plane across the surface. Often the beginner feels that a boat sailing close hauled is going faster but this is because things are a bit more exciting with the boat heeled over and because the wind *appears* to be stronger.

Apparent wind

The *apparent wind* is the term we use to describe the wind speed and direction that we experience on the boat; the wind we feel on our faces and that moves across the sails. Whenever the boat is moving in relation to the land the apparent wind will be different from the *true wind* experienced when tied to the mooring or standing still on the shore nearby. The apparent difference is caused by your own motion, just as on a calm day you still get pummelled by a good blast of air if you stick your head out of the window of a vehicle travelling at some speed.

This gets a bit harder to understand once the wind is blowing across your direction of travel, but let us imagine we are sitting on the roof of a steam train. I did this once in India but you need not go to such lengths and the diagrams in figure 3.7 provide a better angle of view anyway.

The apparent wind acts on sails just the same way as it acts on the smoke of the steam train. From this we can see that the apparent wind is created by a combination of true wind and boat speed and direction and is affected by changes in any of these.

The train in figure 3.7 illustrates the change of apparent wind direction when boat speed increases and decreases, but apparent wind speed changes as well of course. If you are sailing with the wind behind you blowing at 10 *knots* and you are sailing at 5 knots then you will have 5 knots of apparent wind. If you were sailing close hauled at 4 knots in the same wind though, the apparent wind against you would be more like 14 knots. So with the boat heeled over more, with the spray flying and with 14 knots of wind in their hair, the beginner feels that the boat is faster and the wind is stonger than when sailing on a *broad reach*. See figure 3.8.

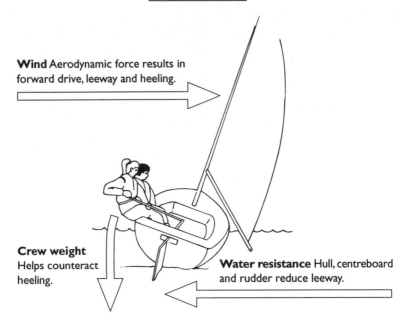

Wind Aerodynamic force results in forward drive, leeway and heeling.

Crew weight
Helps counteract heeling.

Water resistance Hull, centreboard and rudder reduce leeway.

3.6 Balancing the forces.

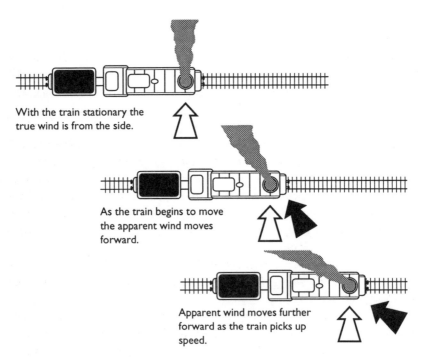

With the train stationary the true wind is from the side.

As the train begins to move the apparent wind moves forward.

Apparent wind moves further forward as the train picks up speed.

3.7 Apparent wind.

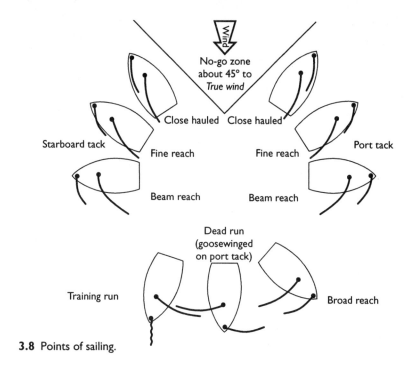

3.8 Points of sailing.

Knots

It was the end of a long passage from Ullapool on the north-west coast of Scotland to Torshaven in the Faeroe Islands. We wanted to get the boat tied up and sorted out so we could get our heads down or explore ashore according to our preferences. It was my first sailing cruise and I was learning as quick as I could but this was the first time we had come in to a pier. There was a flurry of activity on deck as fenders were put over and warps coiled ready to be thrown ashore. I learned that boat people feel very self-conscious when coming in to harbour and they take a pride in manouevring efficiently and with the minimum of fuss. This was even more the case now with a number of Faeroese people on the quay showing interest in our arrival. This, I was told, was to be expected of a seafaring community when a foreign boat arrives and our traditional Danish trawler drew a fair bit of attention.

So plans were made to make neat work of it and as I was considered to be young and nimble I was 'volunteered' to climb the ladder and attend to the shorelines.

As we came alongside and I nipped up the ladder things were going well. The bow line was thrown accurately and I caught it competently but then things began to go wrong. 'Put it on that bollard', said the skipper, pointing. 'How?', I

3.9 Knots.

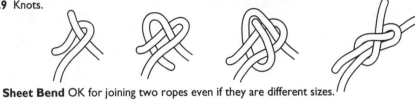

Sheet Bend OK for joining two ropes even if they are different sizes.

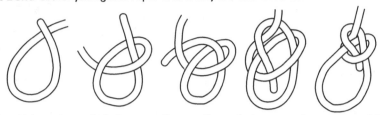

Bowline Makes a loop which does not slip or collapse. An important knot as many jobs can be done with it. Will not untie under load.

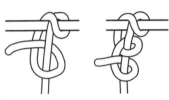

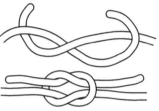

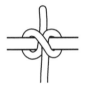

Round turn and two half hitches Good for tying up to a mooring post or ring. Can be undone under load. Can shake loose under jerky load.

Reef knot A flat knot for tying reef points in. Not much good for any other use on board.

Clove hitch A quick fastening onto a post or bar. Cannot be untied under load.

Figure of eight A stopper knot for the end of every sheet and halyard to stop them coming out of their blocks or fairleads.

Buntline hitch For tidying and securing a loose coil of rope.

asked, waving at him the end that I thought would have a loop already tied into it. 'With a bowline', came the inevitable but daunting reply. 'That's the one with the rabbit isn't it?' I retorted, playing for time but with the sinking realization that my incompetence was about to be put on full display. I wondered how many of the onlookers spoke English. Voices were raised slightly and not just in order to cross the widening gap between quay and boat. I continued to fiddle with my end of the rope hoping for a miracle but the wind had already blown the bow away by slightly less than the length of the warp. Fortunately I managed to retain the presence of mind to let go and the boat motored off. I suppose if they had just carried on and sailed off somewhere else I would have been justly repaid, but I was pleased to see them turn around and make another approach. This time the warp that came flying towards me (with perhaps a little more force than was entirely necessary) had a bowline tied firmly in the end of it. The customs officer welcomed himself aboard with a wry smile and I promised myself I would learn to tie a bowline before our next passage.

Your last bit of 'armchair sailing' concerns knots. Ropework is an extremely important aspect of seamanship and it is worth investing some time in learning well. When you do get out and are rigging the dinghy you will find it so much easier and quicker if you have spent a bit of time learning knots in comfort at home and under no pressure from others

Get a piece of rope at least 5mm (⅕in) in diameter and a couple of metres (about 6ft) long. Ideally it should be fairly soft and easy to handle and you should find learning and practising the knots fun and interesting. Like much learning, knots are best remembered when they are used frequently, so keep that piece of rope handy as a source of amusement through those long winter evenings. See figure 3.9.

4

Getting afloat

Who to go with

In Chapter 2 I discussed the merits of starting sailing on an organized course. I feel strongly that you are best off and will learn quickest under competent, qualified instruction at a nationally accredited sailing school.

Some people might comment that as a sailing instructor 'he would say that wouldn't he', and argue that armed with a suitable boat, a good book and an adventurous spirit, you could teach yourself to sail fairly effectively. I would concede that given a reasonable degree of common sense, lots of caution to temper the adventurousness and a good sense of self-preservation you might well have a lot of fun, but I do not believe that you could improve on the aspects of safety and speed of learning that you would experience on a structured course. Most will be good fun as well and you would be sharing laughs with a group of equally incompetent beginners!

It may be however, that you have access to a boat and a bursting desire to try it out by just going on the water and having a go yourself. A word of caution here as it must be realized that there is a possibility (and these things must be considered) that you could end up having a nasty or even fatal accident! I do not want to put a total damper on those keen to get out and 'have a go' but going on the water should always be regarded as a serious undertaking. If you know someone competent who will teach you the basics then you may feel confident to go ahead. If this is the case then you will need thorough preparation and to be very choosy about where you go and in what conditions.

Choosing the conditions

Obviously the conditions you choose for your first attempts at sailing are extremely important and could play a large part in hooking you for life or putting you off altogether. You need a wind that is steady in both speed and direction and unless you are under proper instruction I would recommend for your first session at least that you do not go out in much more than a force 2 on the Beaufort scale. We have all derived learning from various epic adventures and misadventures but there is not a lot of point in starting that way! It can quickly turn from being a bit of fun to an unnerving or frightening experience when things get a bit out of control, and it is essential to appreciate that we are participating in a sport that is usually very safe but can turn dangerous when things go wrong. In a force 2 or less your inevitable early mistakes are unlikely to do damage to you or your boat and you would always be able to row or paddle your boat around if you need to.

Your ability to have a productive first day in conditions which vary from this will depend on the circumstances and on who you are with. If you are feeling confident and under the supervision of an experienced instructor then you would no doubt have a fun and exhilarating time in stronger winds.

The first thing then is to check the weather forecasts in the days leading up to your chosen weekend or day off. There are a huge number of sources of weather information nowadays and they provide the relevant details to varying degrees. Whether it is going to be sunny or not is usually given as the most important, closely followed by the air temperature. Unfortunately the brief forecasts such as 'sunny with a high of 17' are pretty useless as far as we are concerned. So we need something a bit more comprehensive which includes the wind speed as well. This is given either in knots or as a value on the Beaufort scale. The table on page 34 shows a comparison between these and a description of how to judge the wind strength.

It is important that you learn to read the signs of wind strength both ashore and afloat as you cannot just assume that as the forecast indicated a certain wind strength then that is what it is blowing. The actual wind state can vary wildly from the forecast due to local variations, changing conditions and, dare I say, inaccurate forecasting! To be fair it must be said that while satellite observations and computer analysis have greatly improved the methods of recording and processing weather information, the art of prediction is still subject to such a large number of variables that we cannot yet rely on the forecasts to be perfect. The best answer is to develop an understanding of what happens during certain weather fronts and systems and keep a good awareness of the weather changing around you, relating it back to the best information you got from the forecasters. I find this gives me more confidence when the weather is not as forecast and it can help me to work out what else I might expect. It might be that the timing of changes is different or that the track of a depression is not as the

Beaufort force	Description	At sea	On land	Wind speed in knots
Wind strength chart				
0	Calm	Mirror-like.	Smoke rises vertically.	<1
1	Light air	Ripples like scales.	Wind direction shown by smoke but not by wind vanes.	1 to 3
2	Light breeze	Small wavelets. Crests appear glassy and do not break.	Wind felt on face, leaves rustle.	4 to 6
3	Gentle breeze	Large wavelets, crests begin to break.	Leaves and small twigs in constant motion. Wind extends light flags.	7 to 10
4	Moderate breeze	Small waves becoming longer, fairly frequent white horses.	Raises dust and loose paper; small branches are moved.	11 to 16
5	Fresh breeze	Moderate waves, many white horses, chance of some spray.	Small trees in leaf begin to sway. Crested wavelets form on inland waters.	17 to 21
6	Strong breeze	Large waves begin to form; white foam crests are more extensive everywhere. Probably some spray.	Large branches in motion; umbrellas used with difficulty	22 to 27
7	Near gale	Sea heaps up and white foam from breaking crests begins to be blown in streaks along the direction of the wind.	Whole trees in motion; inconvenience when walking against the wind.	28 to 33
8	Gale	Moderately high waves of greater length; edges of crests begin to break into spindrift. Foam is blown in well-marked streaks along the direction of the wind.	Breaks twigs off trees; generally impedes progress.	34 to 40
9	Severe gale	High waves. Crests of waves begin to topple, tumble and roll over. Spray may affect visibility.	Slight structural damage occurs (chimney pots and slates removed).	41 to 47
10	Storm	Very high waves with long overhanging crests. Whole surface takes on a white appearance. Visibility affected.	Seldom experienced inland; trees uprooted; considerable structural damage occurs.	48 to 55

forecasters expected. If you know whether the front has passed yet or whether you expect the wind to go on changing in strength or direction then you are in a better position to make best use of it and avoid conditions you do not want to be out in.

Television

Graphic information can give a good overall impression of weather trends, particularly when a *synoptic chart* is shown. TV forecasts can lack detail of local conditions.

Teletext

This has the advantage of being always available if your television has this facility. Unfortunately they do not usually show a synoptic chart but they normally contain some wind information.

Radio

The radio provides a convenient and portable means of receiving weather information which you can nearly always have with you whether you are driving off to the coast, camping, out for a day's cruise or longer, or just sitting at breakfast at the weekend trying to decide whether to go sailing or not.

The shipping forecasts broadcast in the UK are given out four times a day and cover large areas around the coast of the British Isles stretching to Iceland, Scandinavia and Portugal. They give the locations of the weather systems and predicted and recorded wind directions and Beaufort scale strengths. Once you have learnt how to interpret the information it can give an invaluable overview to the coastal sailor. It must be remembered that the sea areas each cover a large distance out to sea so are not generally intended for the inshore sailor.

Inshore water forecasts are broadcast regularly on local and national stations. These forecasts give a general picture of the weather pattern, predicted wind strengths (usually Beaufort scale) and directions for sections of coastline. The UK national reports usually start at Berwick upon Tweed and proceed clockwise around the UK, naming specific points on the coast to define each area. Unlike the shipping forecast areas which are named and remain the same, the inshore stretches of coastline vary according to the needs of the forecast, so you need a rough idea of where you want to sail and the major landmarks in the coastline in that area.

Inshore waters forecasts are ideal for inshore and coastal sailors in most areas.

Newspapers

Some newspapers are better than others when it comes to providing useful weather information. Their advantage is that they give a chart that you can go back and refer to, even when getting later information on the radio. You should look for a report that also gives wind speed and direction for your local area and preferably an outlook as to how things will change over the next day or so. Pictures of clouds or sunshine are pretty but not as essential from the sailor's point of view!

Telephone

Information for specific coastal areas is available by telephone in some countries. In the UK this service is called Marinecall, a weather information service at premium telephone rates. The pre-recorded information is comprehensive, available at any time and updated twice a day. The numbers relevant to your area and the current rates are advertised in the telephone directory under 'weather services'. Make sure you have a pen ready as the report comes fairly quickly. If you can write in some abbreviated way you may be able to get all the information down without having to listen to it all through again which can be costly.

For details of reports in other countries contact the relevant organizations given in Appendix 1 on page 146.

Fax machine

If you have access to a fax machine then you can also receive weather information by fax. In addition to the written details you can also get current and forecast synoptic charts. It is worth getting an index page listing the services available (and rates). You need to operate your machine in 'poll receive' mode. This is the fax equivalent of a reverse charge where you dial the appropriate number and then receive the fax, paying for it at the premium rate advertised.

Other sources

Users of VHF marine radios are able to receive weather forecasts from the coastguard and shipping forecast repetitions from coast radio stations in the UK. In dinghy sailing as a beginner you are less likely to have access to this equipment however and it is only much later, when considering coastal dinghy cruising perhaps, that it would become worth considering as a good investment.

Checking the tide

The wind and weather conditions are not the only things you need to look up in advance, particularly if you are in a coastal area when it is essential that you know what the tide is doing. Tide times are usually published in local papers or in specific booklets available from chandlers shops and some newsagents. Chapter 8 on basic coastal sailing is essential reading for the beginner starting on tidal water.

Choosing the place

The ideal place for a beginner to sail would have steady light winds unaffected by land influences; no tide or current; an enclosed sailing area of moderate size uncongested by moorings or other boats except for a safety boat and a variety of easy access launching sites. The place you eventually choose to sail will not have all of these features, of course, but you will have to decide what compromise is best. You are not likely to have a rescue boat looking out for you alone but it would be more important to sail where there is one than to go off to some remote spot just to have plenty of room to manoeuvre and make mistakes. You can normally find an area out of other people's way even at times when there is a race on. Etiquette asks you to keep out of the way of boats racing although if you do get close to them the collision regulations do apply (see page 131). It is well worth avoiding areas with strong tidal streams until you are experienced as they complicate matters and can confuse you.

Staying flexible

Having checked your weather and tidal information it is always worth reconsidering your plan and deciding on something appropriate to the conditions. Be prepared not to go if the weather is not to your liking. As you get more experienced you will get a feel for the wind conditions in which you and your boat are happy, those in which you are glad to have the club safety boat on patrol, and those conditions when you would rather not be on the water at all. If you are not sure then ask the advice of someone experienced, take them with you if you can and make sure that help would be at hand if you needed it. In these sort of circumstances you will gradually expand your experience and develop the ability to sail in more testing conditions – an essential skill of the intermediate and developing sailor.

For a recent summer cruise I stayed flexible right to the last minute to try and get the best out of the conditions.

I was enormously relieved that we were finally away. Totally exhausted after a week of ridiculously late nights at the sewing machine finishing off the new boom tent I now felt really pleased as we relaxed in sleeping bags lying quietly to anchor. Christine could not believe I had managed to finish the tent; I was not sure how I had done it myself but there we were and I had a sneaking suspicion that with all the procrastination of not deciding where to go until the last minute, I might just have come up with an ideal plan! It was a bit nerve racking to keep putting off the decision but fortunately with enough charts I had variously begged, borrowed and bought we were able to keep options open and 'make the best possible decision at the last possible moment'! Luckily the high pressure system I had been watching had finally established itself to the north and looked set to stay there for a few days so we launched at Fionnphort on the west side of the island of Mull in Scotland. This can be a treacherous place at the wrong time in a small boat, but get the timing right, and the lochs and islands are some of the most beautiful in Britain. I would never have dared plan a holiday there in a 5m (16ft) open boat and relied on being able to do much, particularly as we were looking for a relaxing stress-free holiday. If I had had to commit myself to a specific launch place well in advance we would probably have gone somewhere else. As it happened though we had some good winds up to force five, blowing offshore so there was no swell, some great sailing and we explored the islands and had lots of sunshine into the bargain.

Let us go back to considering your early sailing career. If you are thinking of sailing on the coast then a light breeze blowing along the shore or a sheltered enclosed bay would be much more appropriate than a fresh offshore wind. If you have a choice, this checklist might help you decide where to launch.

Points to consider when launching:

- Are there tidal constraints?
- Is the slipway usable at all heights of tide?
- Are there strong tidal streams to avoid?
- Is the wind strength suitable? Is it likely to change while you are out?
- Is the wind offshore/blowing off the beach?
- Is the sailing area enclosed or could you get blown out?
- Is there a club rescue boat on patrol?
- If not can someone keep an eye on you from the shore?
- If not who can you tell of your plans?

Preparing the boat

Check that all the equipment, including boat buoyancy and safety equipment, is in good order and look for any signs of defective gear when you get it ready. If you do have your own boat then learn how to keep it in good order. It is worth developing your own checklist of what to remember to take both for the boat and for personal gear. This will help you to get away quickly when setting off and ensure that you do not overlook something essential. My first list for my boat even included things which might sound obvious but which I felt might just get overlooked if I was in a hurry and rummaging around. I am not sure whether putting this in writing is asking for trouble but so far I have never arrived at a slipway having left the mast, boom, sails, rudder or anything that obvious at home. I am sure it is quite possible to do so though, particularly at the beginning of the season, so I am sticking to my checklist system and leaving all those items on it. Here is a list of equipment that you might consider adapting for your own use.

Equipment checklist

	Local sail and short race	Day sailing and coastal
Personal equipment	Buoyancy aid with whistle attached Clothing suitable for the conditions Inner layers Wetsuit Wet shoes/boots Cagoule Waterproof trousers Hat Gloves Sunscreen Sunglasses Swimming costume Sailing knife A few bits of spare cord and a couple of spare shackles Things to have ashore: Towel and shower gear, dry clothes to change into.	*Add:* Extra spare clothing, waterproofed in poly bag. Lunch / food /snacks Flask / drink Full life-jackets

	Local sail and short race	Day sailing and coastal
Boat's equipment	Mast, boom, rudder, tiller, sails, sheets. Bailer Bungs Buoyancy bags Painter Paddles/oars and crutches	Warps Fenders Flare pack Basic tool kit: pliers, screwdriver, adjustable spanner. Spare shackles. First aid kit Chart/map Compass Lead line Anchor and chain or warp flaked into bucket

Trolleys and trailers

Having decided on your plan and checked your gear over you will need to get the boat to the water. Ideally you will have it tied up on a nice stretch of placid non-tidal water at the bottom of your garden and can just stroll down, jump in and hoist the sails. That is my particular fantasy anyway, but as we live in the real world you will probably have to move it on land to get to the water. For this clearly you will need wheels and generally these fall into two categories: trolleys and road trailers.

Trolleys are designed to enable you to manoeuvre the boat for short distances when close to the water. They are simple with a minimum of parts that can rust but are not suitable for use on the road. If you plan to keep the dinghy in one place and just need to be able to wheel it down the slipway then a trolley is all you need. This may be from a club compound for example but you will still have to overcome the problem of delivering your boat to its home in the first place.

Road trailers are designed to travel at speed along the road and therefore require bearings to reduce the friction and allow the wheels to turn freely without getting too hot. The wheels may be sprung and heavier dinghy trailers are likely to have a winch to help recover the boat from the water. The next step up in the weight bracket also has brakes but most boats up to 5m (16ft) or so are not heavy enough to require a braked trailer. Obviously having a road trailer can increase the scope of your sport and will give you the option of choosing your launch site. The disadvantage is that the good ones are expensive and the features that make them suitable for road use are rather susceptible to rust. This is particularly problematic if you use them to launch in sea water and it is necessary to immerse the wheels. The more expensive of the larger boat trailers minimize the effect of this or avoid it altogether by a variety of means. The best answer is to have both. A 'piggy back' or combination trailer keeps its road wheels out of the water by carrying a separate trolley which you wheel off to launch the boat.

Another type I have seen used with the heavier trailed boats is the break-back trailer. This works by changing the angle of the bed of the trailer so that the boat can be winched on and off at a better angle with the trailer just in shallow water. The boat is supported and guided by rollers as it is winched into position. My trailer for my heavy 5m (16ft) boat has rollers at the back end which make it easy to locate the boat on to the trailer correctly even if I am recovering it on my own.

If you do have a road trailer which needs to be immersed then the wheel bearings should be of the sealed variety. About the worst thing you can do to a set of trailer wheels is to immerse them in salt water and then let them stand for a while to allow the salt water to seep in around the bearings, This of course is exactly what you would do every time you trail and launch the boat but if you can find the time to hose the wheels off in fresh water and go for a short drive to help dispel the salt and dry things out a bit then your bearings should last longer. Check your bearings regularly and re-pack the hubs with grease when needed. When storing your trailer for any length of time (and particularly over the winter) it is worth lifting the weight off the wheels by supporting the axle with blocks. This helps the tyres stay in better shape and in my case gets them out of the rather soggy ground that they would otherwise sit in.

The best trailers and trolleys are galvanized but even then rust seems to attack them. If you have a winch, keep it greased and covered as the galvanizing seems to wear off these moving parts more quickly. I learnt how not to look after a trailer the hard way a few years ago when I was driving off on the way to a launch site for a summer cruise.

We had not really made much progress by lunchtime. The inevitable last minute changes and additions to our kit delayed our departure. I felt pretty satisfied on the whole and with bright sunshine, the car pulling nicely and the boat looking well prepared, we were all in a good mood as we headed up the Great Glen in the Scottish Highlands. Unfortunately these feelings of smug satisfaction can often precede a downfall of some degree and this was to prove one of my worst, compounded by the fact that two friends were along to witness my stupidity and increase my embarrassment.

As the trailer gouged its way to a halt and the nearside wheel overtook us on its way into a ditch I knew we were in for rather a long lunch stop. We spent a considerable time looking for a missing hub cap then put the wheel back on to see if we could limp anywhere. It looked hopeless so I made my way up to a nearby hotel while the others tucked in to the best of the picnic. I was pleasantly surprised to hear that my breakdown insurers were going to be quite helpful and some time later was relieved to see the trailer wobble its way up on to the ramps of the recovery truck. By this time I had decided to rescue the holiday plans as much as possible and phoned around to check out a garage near our intended launch site. It was dark by the time the trailer wobbled its way back off the truck and it was the following morning before we could launch the boat so the local garage could deal with the trailer. A charmingly helpful couple had let us camp in their garden and in the end we only sailed off about half a day behind schedule. A successful cruise followed but the garage bill and the gentle ribbing of friends has helped to remind me to service my trailer more regularly since then.

Rigging the boat

Checklist for rigging and launching a boat:

- Step the mast
- Check all equipment is aboard and secure
- Prepare mainsail, mainsheet and kicking strap
- Hoist jib
- Hoist mainsail only if wind is blowing offshore
- Launch
- Fit rudder and tiller
- (Hoist mainsail if not yet done)
- Insert daggerboard/partially lower centreboard if water is deep enough
- Go!

If you keep the boat at the water's edge then the mast can remain in place all season but if you have trailed the boat to your chosen site you will need to step the mast before launching. Masts either step down into the bottom of the boat (keel stepped) or on to a fitting at deck level. Most are stayed with wire rigging (see figure 4.1) but some, particularly single-handers like the Laser and Topper, just fit down into a slot and are unsupported.

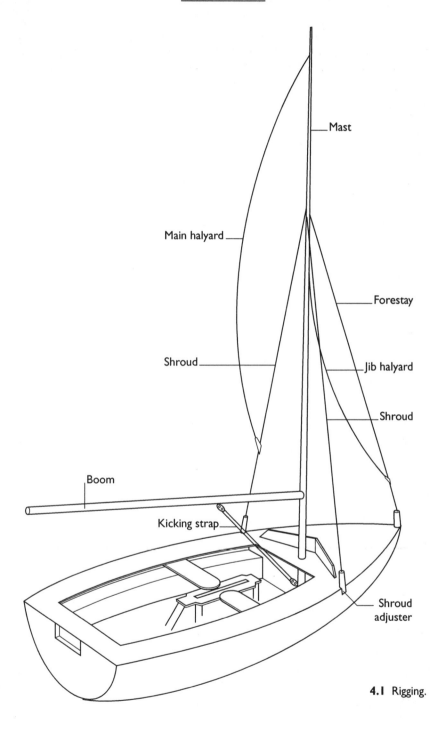

Mast

Main halyard

Forestay

Shroud

Jib halyard

Shroud

Boom

Kicking strap

Shroud
adjuster

4.1 Rigging.

The best way to step the mast will depend on the particular boat and whether the mast is keel stepped or deck stepped. It is usually best to attach at least one of the rigging wires – either the forestay or the shrouds, before trying to raise the mast. This will help to hold the mast upright while the rest of the rigging is fixed in place. The main point to avoid is trying to balance a tall mast upright with nothing helping to support it. It could then easily topple over which potentially could cause damage.

With the mast stepped we turn our attention to the rest of the rigging.

It is worth hoisting the *mainsail* on shore at least the first time to become familiar with how to do it. The boat must be pointing into the wind on its trolley to do this so that the sail does not fill with wind which might make the boat sail along on its trolley thereby causing difficulties in handling or damage in stronger winds. It is not usually possible to leave the mainsail hoisted right through the launching process unless the wind very light or is blowing straight down the slipway and offshore. If it is offshore then you can keep the boat head to wind all the way down the slipway and into the water. Otherwise keep the main lowered until the boat is in the water and pointing head to wind. (See page 52 for the main exception to this with unstayed mast types.)

Usually the following order of events is best, sorting as much as possible out before any sails are raised so they do not flog around for ages waiting for something to happen. This can cause damage to the sail in stronger winds, in which case it may be better to launch first and then hoist the sails once afloat.

Hoisting the jib
Shackle the bottom front corner (*tack*) of the jib to the fitting on the bow of the boat and sort out the *sheets*. These are the ropes that control the angle of the sail to the wind and are attached to the bottom back corner of the sail (*clew*). Follow the bottom edge (*foot*) of the sail along, making sure there are no twists. Then pass each of the two sheets either side down the boat and through the *fairleads*. A figure-of-eight knot is then tied in each of the ends to stop the sheet from coming out of the fairlead. Near the fairlead is usually a type of *jamming cleat* which allows the sheet to be easily adjusted without the crew having to hold it all the time (see figure 3.1). The sheets need not be cleated yet as once the sail is up you want it to flap loosely, spilling wind until you sail off.

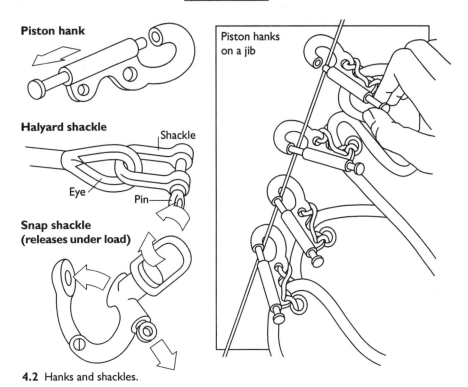

4.2 Hanks and shackles.

From here the technique differs according to the arrangement you have on your boat. Some larger dinghies have *piston hanks* that clip on to the forestay. With these it is usual to work from the tack up to the *head* of the sail, clipping them on without putting a twist in the sail. You will soon see if you have done it right when you hoist the sail. The rope or wire which will hoist the sail is called the jib halyard. Look up to check it is not twisted around the *shrouds* and attach the halyard to the top corner (head) of the sail (this is usually done with a small *shackle*), then hoist last of all.

Once the halyard comes tight then it can be *swigged* up to ensure a taut *luff* which is essential for sailing close to the wind.

Many modern performance dinghies do not have the jib hanked on to the forestay at all. This is because with a wire luff and halyard the sail does not need the support of the forestay and is set up independently. When this is the case extra tension can be gained by one person pulling out on the forestay when the last of the halyard is being taken in. This has the effect of pulling the mast forward slightly, allowing the jib luff to set tighter once the forestay is released again. There are a

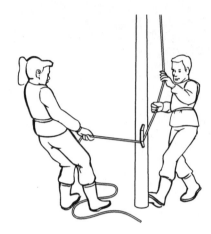

4.3 Swigging up a halyard.

variety of types of cleat for securing the halyard but the most common are shown in figure 4.4.

Preparing the mainsail

Loose-footed sails do not slide into a boom groove but just attach at the tack to the front end of the boom and at the clew with the *outhaul*.

A sail with some belly in it creates more drive so in stronger winds flatten the sail by stretching the foot tight with the outhaul.

With the boom lying in the boat fold the sail down on top of it ensuring that the *luff* or front edge is not twisted. The mainsail is now ready to hoist once you are afloat or pointed head to wind. It is a good idea to do this ashore the first time so that you can get familiar with how things work. You may have to lower it again to launch the boat so once you are familiar with it you would usually leave hoisting it until you are afloat.

Hoisting the mainsail

Make sure the boat is pointing into the wind. Find the main halyard and look up to check it is not caught up around the shrouds or twisted. Shackle it to the top corner or head of the sail, then pull on the halyard as you feed the luff of the sail into the groove in the mast.

Once the sail is beginning to take the weight of the boom then it should be supported as the last of the halyard is taken up. The forward end of the boom fits on to the mast with a fitting called a *gooseneck*. Some larger dinghies have a *topping lift*, which is a rope running up and down the mast a bit like a halyard but is attached to the boom to

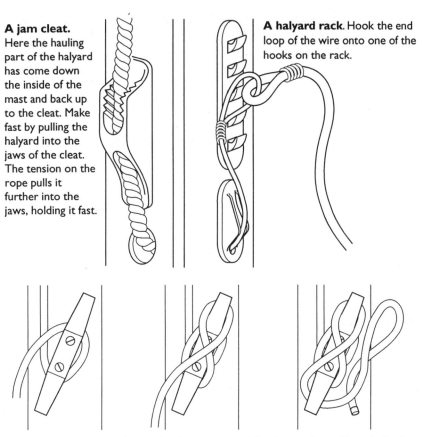

A jam cleat.
Here the hauling part of the halyard has come down the inside of the mast and back up to the cleat. Make fast by pulling the halyard into the jaws of the cleat. The tension on the rope pulls it further into the jaws, holding it fast.

A halyard rack. Hook the end loop of the wire onto one of the hooks on the rack.

An ordinary cleat. Take figure-of-eight turns around the cleat as shown. Here the hauling part of the halyard is led down the outside of the mast.

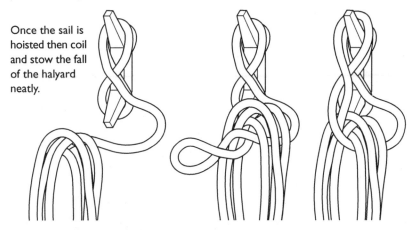

Once the sail is hoisted then coil and stow the fall of the halyard neatly.

4.4 Securing the jib halyard.

4.5 Attaching the foot of the sail to the boom.

Boom groove

Tack

1. Many booms have a groove which the foot of the sail slides into, working from the forward end of the boom.

2. The tack is then secured at the forward end of the boom, usually with a pin.

3. The clew is lashed or pulled back with the outhaul.

Outhaul

support its weight when the sail is not fully raised. The mainsheet should be slack at this stage with the mainsail free to swing across the boat so it does not catch the wind. Mind your head!

The mainsail luff tension is often controlled by a *cunningham*. This is usually a simple cord which leads from the lower part of the mast, up to the sail and through an eye near the bottom of the luff back down the mast again to a jam cleat. Other types have a sliding gooseneck which can be pulled down to increase the luff tension.

The last thing to sort out on the mainsail is the kicking strap. This is a tackle that clips into the underside of the boom and can be adjusted to change the shape of the sail (see figure 3.2). Do not pull it tight at the moment, however, as this can limit the boom and you want it free to swing.

Variations

There are so many different sorts of boat and different combinations of rig that it would not be worth trying to detail them all in a beginner's guide. There are variations to those detailed above which you might come across. So I will mention two which although at opposite ends of the spectrum are becoming more popular.

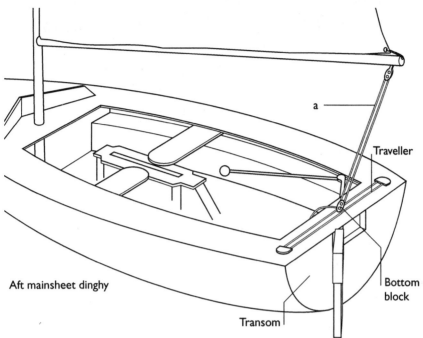

a

Traveller

Aft mainsheet dinghy

Bottom block

Transom

Aft mainsheet (a) runs from the after end of the boom down to the transom where it is attached to the traveller (usually a piece of rope or wire fixed across the transom along which the mainsheet block runs). Tie a figure-of-eight stopper knot in the end of the sheet to keep it in the block. Dinghies for higher performance or racing tend to have a centre mainsheet (b) which allows better sail control but takes up more space than the aft mainsheet common in general purpose and cruising dinghies.

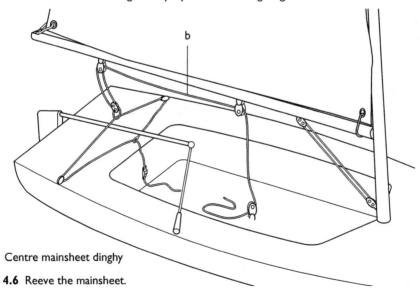

b

Centre mainsheet dinghy

4.6 Reeve the mainsheet.

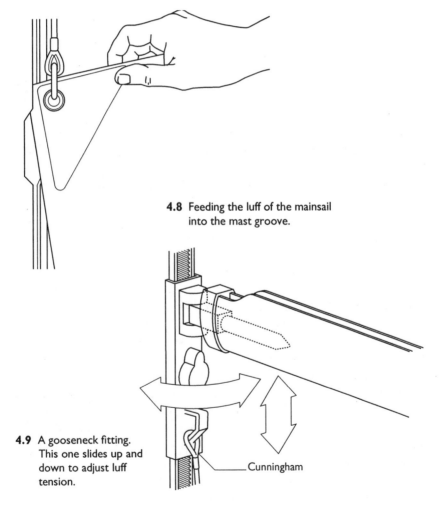

4.7 Fitting the sail battens. These are made of plastic or wood and fit into pockets in the sail to help it hold its shape.

4.8 Feeding the luff of the mainsail into the mast groove.

4.9 A gooseneck fitting. This one slides up and down to adjust luff tension.

Cunningham

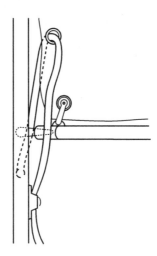

4.10 A simple cunningham.

Gunter and gaff rig

With these more traditional rigs the mast is shorter than that of the equivalent bermudan rigged boat, the sail being extended higher by an additional spar called a *gaff*. The main advantage on a trailing boat is that the shorter mast is then easier to deal with and often fits within the length of the boat. On the other hand the tall luff or leading edge of the bermudan rig gives a better performance to windward and so is generally favoured in racing boats. When choosing your boat you will have to decide on your own priorities. The more traditional styles are making a comeback nowadays, particularly for cruising, and many people enjoy the sheer beauty of the traditional boat despite the lesser performance.

The Outward Bound cutters are about 9m (28ft) long, traditionally rigged with gaff or lugsails and attract a fair amount of attention when out from their various bases. The gunter is a modern descendant of the gaff rig really, the main difference being that with the gunter rig the extra spar (still called a *gaff*) is set at a steeper angle, effectively extending the mast. With a gaff rig the gaff is set at a shallower angle, often allowing another sail, a topsail, to be set in the triangle created between the gaff and the top of the main mast. The edge of the sail that lies along the gaff is called the *head* on these four-sided sails. It is either fed into a groove in the gaff, similar to a typical boom groove, or is laced to it. The top corner of the gaff and gunter sail is now called the *peak* and is attached to the corresponding top end of the gaff, usually by lacing. The foot of the sail is then attached to the boom, much the same way as described in the previous section. These sails are often

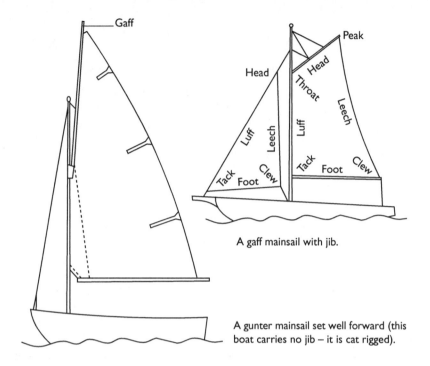

A gaff mainsail with jib.

A gunter mainsail set well forward (this boat carries no jib – it is cat rigged).

4.11 Gaff and gunter rigs.

loose footed although sometimes they are laced to the boom. In dinghies the luff of gaff and gunter sails is usually laced to the mast as the sail is hoisted. Gaff rigged boats usually have two halyards one for the peak and one for the *throat*, allowing the angle of the gaff to be set so eliminating creases in the sail.

Unstayed masts

Modern small single-handed dinghies tend to have much simpler rigs with a single sail. Modern materials allow a strong lightweight and flexible mast which sits in a slot in the foredeck and does not require forestay or shrouds to support it. The mainsail is sleeved over the mast so you slide it on before you step the mast. This is then a simple process of standing the mast upright on the ground, lifting it vertically and lowering it into the slot. As there are no shrouds to restrict the sail it can be left to flap freely downwind during the launch. It may be necessary to delay attaching the sail to the boom with the outhaul until the boat is afloat head to wind.

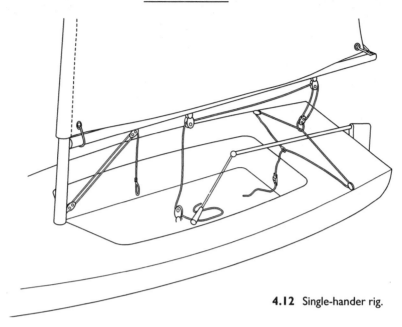

4.12 Single-hander rig.

Launching

You will get quicker at preparing the boat for the water but you will probably be itching to get afloat by now. Take care with the trolley on the slipway though. They tend to be just that, particularly at low tide when the exposed section is rather slimy. I have seen many a person take a flyer on a slipway despite being told to take care. It must be the excitement of getting close to the water that goes to their heads so make sure you do not put an early stop to your first day before you have even got on the water. You have been warned!

Back the boat down the slipway using as many people as it needs to make sure it does not run away with you. Have a *painter* ready, attached to the bow of the boat and tied off on the trailer. At the water's edge keep going until the boat floats off the trailer, but keep hold of the painter. One person then stands in the water holding the bow of the dinghy, letting the boat blow downwind and keeping it in enough water to float. You should avoid heaving the dinghy off before it floats or allowing it to ground on the slipway as this can damage the hull surface. If the wind is blowing *onshore* the crew may be standing quite deep so do not take too long to put the trolley away somewhere out of the way of the slip and above the reach of the tide. Returning to the clubhouse for a last slurp of tea is not popular at this stage so you should return quickly to finish the preparations and make your getaway.

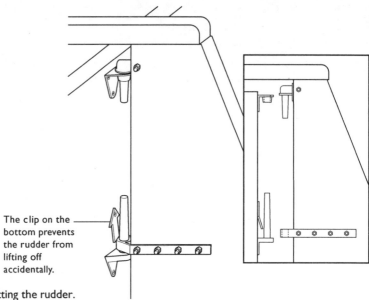

The clip on the bottom prevents the rudder from lifting off accidentally.

4.13 Fitting the rudder.

Now is the time to fit the rudder into its fittings on the stern of the boat. Many boats which have lifting rudders can be launched with the rudder on but it is best to leave it until you are afloat if you are not sure. The tiller is the rod coming into the boat that controls the rudder. Another rod called a tiller extension swivels from the end of the tiller and allows the helmsman to steer whilst sitting out to the side of the boat for balance. The tiller/rudder assembly is usually tied on to the boat in some way, often just by the lifting and lowering cord. You will probably have to keep the rudder blade lifted until you set off and are in slightly deeper water.

The mainsail can be hoisted at this stage (if you do not have it up already) and you can loosely attach the kicking strap. It is best not to tighten the kicking strap yet as this may prevent the mainsail from spilling wind easily. It is important to have the sheets slack and the sails spilling wind until you set off, otherwise the crew ends up fighting the boat and it tries to start sailing.

Finally insert the daggerboard into its case and lower it far enough for the top of it to clear the boom as it swings. If you have a centre-board then it is easier to lower that down when you need it so just make sure the control lines are not tied up in knots. All being well you should be ready to sail off now and how you do that will depend on the wind direction.

Sailing away from a beach
Wind blowing along the shore

This is the most simple scenario for sailing off a beach as all you do is push off in the right direction and start sailing. Check that the area you plan to sail into is free of boats and moorings or walk the dinghy along the beach a little if you need a bit more room. With the crew holding the dinghy head to wind with the sails raised and flapping freely, the helmsman sits in the boat ready with tiller and *mainsheet*. When both are ready the crew moves along to the shroud, pushes the bow away from the beach and climbs aboard. He or she should then sheet in the *leeward jib sheet* to get the boat sailing and help it *bear away* from the wind. Then partly lower the centreboard, further adjusting it as needed.

The helmsman steers the boat away from the beach, lowers the rudder and sheets the mainsail in once they are sailing in the right direction. It is best not to sheet in the mainsail until the crew is aboard and jib sheeted otherwise it will tend to bring the boat back up towards the wind or *luff up*.

Wind blowing offshore

With the wind offshore the main consideration is to choose in which direction to sail off. The crew will be holding the bow of the boat and it will be pointing roughly towards the beach, sails flapping freely. As you will not have mastered sailing backwards yet you will be wanting to turn the boat and sail it forwards away from the beach. Decide therefore which direction gives you most room and plan a route that allows you to sail across the wind giving a wide berth to any obstacles.

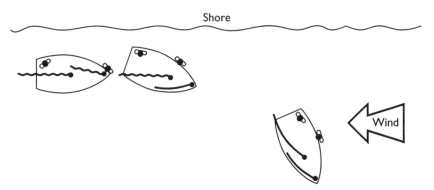

4.14 Sailing away from the beach with the wind blowing along the shore.

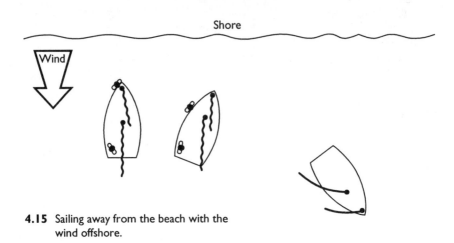

Shore

Wind

4.15 Sailing away from the beach with the wind offshore.

The helmsman climbs in and lowers the rudder as much as is possible and when both are ready the crew gives the bow a good shove away from the beach in the right direction and clambers in. With the boat thus turned away from the beach you can happily sail off in the right direction.

Leave the mainsheet and the centreboard until you are sailing otherwise it will be harder for the boat to turn away from the wind and the shore.

Wind blowing onshore

If the wind is blowing onshore things can be a little more difficult. Firstly you will probably have launched without the mainsail up so the crew will be standing in deeper water holding on to the bow of the boat as you hoist the mainsail. Secondly there may be some small waves coming in to the shore to add to the difficulty. In the light winds you will be learning in this may not be too much of a problem but further on in your sailing career you may find yourself sailing from a beach where waves are a significant problem in onshore winds. Thirdly you will need to make progress upwind to get away from the beach and this is just when you will most need the centreboard. This proves a little difficult when the water is shallow and the waves make it worse. Basically, as an old hand once said to me, 'If you're not sure of getting off the beach happily then you're even less likely to make a good job of coming ashore again.' In other words stay flexible and avoid difficult conditions until either you are experienced enough to cope or you can take someone along with you who can show you how.

4.16 Sailing away from the beach with the wind blowing onshore.

In light winds, with only small waves if any, you should be able to manage, particularly if the beach soon drops off deep enough to lower the centreboard fully. Plan your route off, avoiding obstacles and shallows and making best use of the wind direction if it suggests a preferred *tack*. You will need to be sharp at getting the boat sailing well against the wind otherwise you will rapidly end up back on the beach!

Once the sails are up, lower the centreboard and rudder as far as possible and give some encouragement to the crew who may be standing waist deep in the water! When both of you are ready the crew moves to what will become the windward shroud and in a fluid movement pushes the bow off in the direction required and jumps in. The mainsail should be sheeted in immediately and the centreboard and rudder lowered as much as possible as you sail into deeper water.

Rowing and paddling

Another way of dealing with the onshore wind problem is to launch the boat with sails down and then row off and pick up a mooring or anchor temporarily. Some dinghies are kept on a mooring so you may need to row a smaller boat to get out to it. If this is the case then take the opportunity to row yourself out rather than get a lift in a motor boat or be rowed by someone else. It is good practice and an important skill to develop as you are bound to need it sooner or later. The safety boat can then be just that and only help out if you are having trouble. If you are somewhere without safety cover then you should already be able to row confidently. If you are uncertain about the wind and tide conditions then you must ask yourself whether you should be going on the water at all that day.

More traditional open dinghies usually row quite well and often come equipped with a pair of *oars* and *crutches* (popularly referred to as *rowlocks* although this is really what you call the socket that they fit into). Sit on the centre *thwart* (seat) facing the stern and keep the boat balanced by spreading out the weight of people and gear evenly. If you are rowing a sailing dinghy then make sure the boom and sails are out of your way. It is inadvisable to row with the mainsail hoisted until you are more aware of approaching gusts of wind which can catch you out by heeling the boat over suddenly. In any case in centre mainsheet boats the mainsheet often gets in the way of the oars.

When rowing, stretch your legs out, feet apart to help balance and brace·you. Concentrate on making effective strokes with the oars, putting them in the water fully and pulling evenly. Going in a straight line takes a bit of practice but is more important than going fast.

Keep an eye over your shoulder to check where you are going or get the person sitting in the stern to point. Either way look at the shore *astern* to try and hold a straight line and correct your course by pulling more on one side than the other. Getting to know which oar to pull on to straighten up comes after a little experience. Try picking a point dead astern and see which way it moves when you go off course. If you start looking to the left to keep your eye on it then it is the left hand oar you need to pull on harder to correct. Try to become aware of the effect the wind has on the boat and how it blows you off course. The section on tidal stream and transits in Chapter 8 should help with this.

As you come up alongside another boat you should *stow* the nearest crutch and oar to avoid the danger of damaging the surface of the other hull. A well-handled dinghy never comes into contact with another boat but is held a few inches away when you are transferring across. If you need to tie it alongside for a while to unload then some sort of *fendering* should be used which acts as a cushion between the two hulls.

If you are rowing an inflatable then with most of the dinghy above the water it is even more affected by wind and gets blown off course easily. Shorter quick strokes seem to work more effectively with inflatables as they tend to have shorter oars.

If the boat does not have oars then it should be equipped with at least one paddle which can be used by the crew sitting just behind the shrouds. The helmsman sits on the other side of the boat to balance and steers with the tiller. If you have two paddles then you can paddle from either side of the boat, balancing each other's efforts to keep straight. If you are on your own then the easiest way to keep in a straight line in many boats is to kneel in the stern, remove the rudder and paddle it stern first.

Modern single-handers are usually taken out without a paddle but then are sailed within sight of a safety boat. They can be *sculled* for short distances by waggling the tiller from side to side. This technique also works on larger boats but gets tiring rapidly and can damage the rudder fittings so should not be relied on to cover any distance. If you were really needing to get anywhere you might do better to remove the daggerboard or rudder and use it as a makeshift paddle.

Sailing from a mooring

So far we have looked at launching the dinghy from a slipway or beach, but some dinghies are kept on moorings or even on a pontoon or jetty. If the boat is at a mooring then it will be usually sitting head to wind, but if the tide is strong it will point into it. This should not be the case for your early sessions but the technique is useful when you progress to sailing in tidal streams and more difficult sailing conditions.

Leaving a mooring – head to wind

In this case both sails can be raised and with the sheets out they will be flapping freely. Lower the rudder and centreboard and get the mooring line ready to slip. Check the area you plan to sail into, being aware of how any tide will affect you once you have cast off, back the jib (see page 70) and let go the mooring. Once the boat is heading more across the wind you can *trim* the sails and then alter for your intended course.

Leaving a mooring – wind against tide

In a strong tide with a light wind blowing the opposite way you may well be lying head to tide. Even if this is not quite the case and you seem to be lying across the tide, if the wind is anywhere aft of the beam then this is the method to use. This is because you would not be able to hoist the mainsail without it filling with wind so the jib alone is hoisted while you are on the mooring. Lower the rudder and a little centre-board, get the mooring line ready to slip and have the mainsail ready to hoist. Check the area you plan to sail into and with the jib flapping let go of the mooring. You will then drift back off the mooring and can sheet in the jib and sail clear. When you have plenty of room, lower the

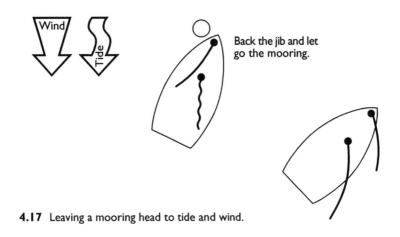

Back the jib and let go the mooring.

4.17 Leaving a mooring head to tide and wind.

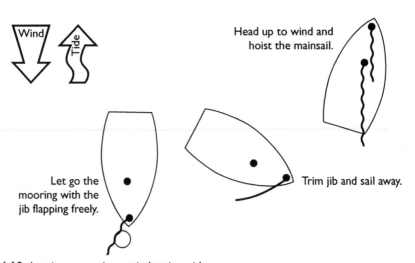

Head up to wind and hoist the mainsail.

Let go the mooring with the jib flapping freely.

Trim jib and sail away.

4.18 Leaving a mooring – wind against tide.

centreboard, turn up to wind, let the jib fly, hoist the mainsail then trim sails and adjust centreboard for your intended point of sailing.

Leaving a pontoon or jetty

Sailing off a pontoon requires the same considerations as leaving a mooring with regard to the wind and tide strength and direction. An advantage that you do have is that you can walk the boat along to a different position or just turn it around using *warps,* the ropes used to tie boats up. Its perfectly seamanlike to make use of this in order to make life easier, and until you have reached the stage when you like to set yourself harder challenges, just go for the simple solutions.

There are obviously a huge number of scenarios possible but the following should prompt you to come up with at least one idea that should solve the problem.

A cannot raise the mainsail with the wind behind and must turn the boat around to sail off.

B is a bit short of space and moves to another position to sail off.

C can hoist both sails, lower the centreboard, push off the bow and go.

D has to be careful that the boom and sails clear the pontoon as they fly. If this were a higher jetty or wall then the mainsail could not be hoisted in this position and D would have to move elsewhere to sail off.

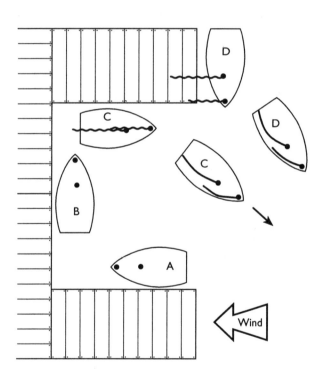

4.19 Leaving a pontoon, onshore wind.

A can hoist both sails and might have room to back the jib, fall away from the wind and bear away to sail clear with centreboard only slightly lowered. Alternatively they could move back and hang off the pontoon with the painter taken from the bow, through a cleat on the pontoon and back to the boat. When ready the crew could back the jib, cast off one end of the painter and pull in on the other end to recover it.

B is a little short of space but with jib only hoisted could cast off the bow line and let the boat turn to face the way out. Sheet in the jib, slip the stern line and sail off into clear water to hoist the mainsail head to wind.

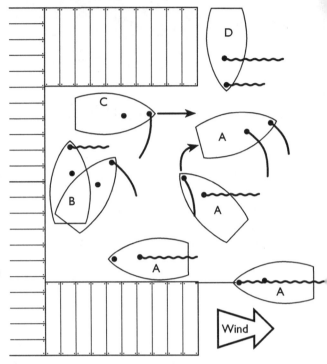

C can simply hoist the jib and sail off again into clear water to hoist the main. If there is not enough space to do this then C will have to turn the boat around and use one of A's techniques.

D can hoist both sails and sail off.

4.20 Leaving a pontoon, offshore wind.

Once there is a tide flowing past or through the pontoons then the situation calls for more experience and a good ability to predict how the tide will affect your boat. For this reason I will assume that you will set off from somewhere simpler at first and deal with sailing in strong tides in Chapter 8.

5

Plain sailing

This chapter concentrates on the basic techniques involved in sailing a given course and making the boat work for you. It follows a progression in the same way that you would on a sailing course but covers all the points of sailing in a series of sections. When practising the skills it is best at first to concentrate on one or two at a time. This helps to focus on the details and makes it easier to learn and progress. No single aspect of sailing can be taken in complete isolation though so you will probably find you will be referring back to previous chapters to refer to points of sailing and sailing away from a beach, working on skills in this chapter, landing ashore again (see Chapter 6), then repeating the process. This sort of method of learning allows you to concentrate on specifics and will also give you plenty of landing and sailing off practice. It also allows you a chance every now and then to get a hot drink or an ice cream depending on the weather and of course refer to the book without getting it too wet!

Reaching – sailing across the wind

Once afloat it is best to find a direction to sail in where you are heading with the wind blowing roughly across the side of the boat. Before we start to think about what the sails are doing it is important that both helmsman and crew are aware of how to balance the boat. You should try to keep the boat upright as much as possible and you use your combined body weights to achieve this. For the helmsman it is best to sit on the same side of the boat that the wind is coming from (*windward*), with your back to the wind and your toes hooked under the *toestraps*. This allows you to lean out when necessary to keep the boat level. The crew will position themselves according to what is needed to keep the boat level. This could be anywhere from leaning out hard to windward in a good breeze, to crouching over on the leeward side in light winds.

When helming hold the mainsheet in the forward hand and the tiller extension in your back hand. This is the same whether the boat has the mainsheet in the centre of the boat or if it is an aft mainsheet which goes to a block on the transom at the back of the boat. The crew controls the jib sheet and the centreboard which for reaching should be about half raised. In order to use the sails most effectively we have to constantly consider sail trim. To trim the sails you hold a steady course and let the sheet out until the front edge (luff) of the sail just starts to flap. At this stage just sheet in until the flapping (luffing) stops and no more. Having done that with both sails they are now trimmed correctly but that is not the end of that job. As your speed increases so the apparent wind will change and wind shifts might cause the sails to need trimming again.

While all this is happening you should be getting the hang of the tiller and steering a steady course. Find a clear stretch of water as the next thing we will do is see how to stop the boat.

Lying to

Try letting both the sheets all the way out so the sails just flap freely. If the mainsail is all the way out and does not flap it will be because it is up against the shrouds and will not go further out to spill wind. In this case you will have to push the tiller away from you to turn the boat a bit more towards the wind until the mainsail also flaps freely. As the sails are no longer producing any drive the boat will come to rest with them flapping freely in the wind. You can let go of the tiller as well and you will find the boat will look after itself *lying to* with the wind blowing across it. It is an important basic skill as in this position you can change places, give yourself a bit of time to think, or sort out a problem. The boat will sit there happily but drift sideways so do not forget to keep an eye on where you are. Lowering the centreboard will slow the amount of drift and raising it fully will allow the boat to drift sideways even more. This is an ideal position for you to first take over the helm, underlining the importance of having someone experienced to go out with at first.

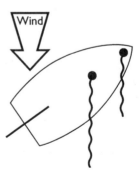

5.1 The lying-to position with both sheets free and the helm let go.

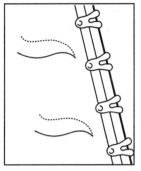
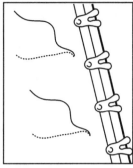
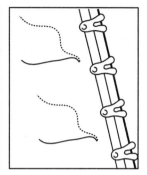

Sail trim is correct when both telltales stream aft.

Sheet in when the windward telltale lifts.

Sheet out when the leeward telltale lifts.

5.2 Telltales.

Forward hand pulls sheet up and across your body.

Then grip sheet with your thumb on tiller extension while other hand lets go and takes hold again further aft.

5.3 Sheeting-in – aft mainsheet.

Sheet in with forward hand. Other hand swings tiller extension down to catch hold of sheet near the block.

Then swing tiller extension back up and aft, keeping hold of sheet. Free forward hand reaches down to grasp sheet near the block ready to repeat sequence.

5.4 Sheeting-in – centre mainsheet.

From this position try pulling in the sheet of each sail in turn and you will see how the sails affect the way the boat turns. Sheeting in just the jib will make the boat *bear away* from the wind; sheeting in just the mainsail will make the boat turn up into the wind (called luffing up). Back in the lying-to position pick another spot to aim for and get ready to sail off again.

Check the area you are going to sail into and gradually bring in the mainsheet. As the boat accelerates keep the main and the jib trimmed and steer a steady course on a beam reach with the wind blowing about 90 degrees across the boat. Make only small movements on the tiller to keep the boat sailing smoothly. Try luffing up towards the wind a little more on to a *close reach*. You will need to sheet in to trim the sails again and do not forget to balance the boat and lower the centreboard more. This point of sailing is a good one to practise your sail trim so make a few small course adjustments and trim the sails accordingly. You may have *telltales* to help with your jib trim. They are short lengths of ribbon or wool attached to each side of the sail a short way back from the luff (see figure 5.2).

Use the method shown in figure 5.3 (or 5.4) to trim the mainsail while steering with the tiller extension.

Next try bearing away from the wind back to a beam reach but do not yet go further than this. The mainsail and jib should be trimmed and the centreboard brought back to about half-way up.

Think now about the fore and aft level of the boat. This is called boat trim and is important to make the boat move efficiently through the water. Generally in light winds and sailing to windward you sit a little further forward to avoid dragging the flat stern of the boat through the water. When in a later session you sail downwind you will sit a little further aft to keep the bow up out of the waves and to help the boat plane in stronger winds.

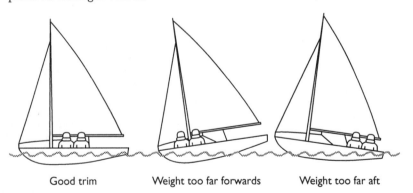

Good trim   Weight too far forwards   Weight too far aft

5.5 Boat trim.

Tacking – turning the boat through the wind, bow upwind

You will, of course, at some stage have to turn the boat around and head back to where you came from with the wind on the other side of the boat. It is best in your first sessions to do this by turning the bow of the boat into the wind and continue turning until you sail off in the new direction. This is called tacking. While you are considering whether to tack make sure you keep the boat sailing, as if you come to a stop the boat will not be able to turn. Practise tacking first by sailing from beam reach to beam reach. The technique differs according to your mainsheet arrangement.

Aft mainsheet tacking

The person on the helm checks that the intended new course will take them clear of any obstructions or other boats and calls 'ready about'. He or she then changes hands on the mainsheet and tiller extension.

The crew also checks for obstructions and if clear replies 'ready', making sure that the jib sheet is ready and not in a tangle or caught up. Figure 5.6 shows what happens next.

Once the boom and the sails have crossed right over to the other side of the boat then the crew can sheet in the jib on the new side and the helmsman can centre the tiller and steer the new course, trimming the mainsail.

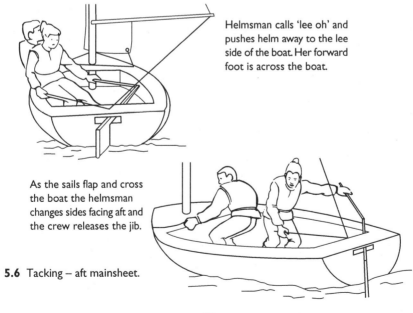

Helmsman calls 'lee oh' and pushes helm away to the lee side of the boat. Her forward foot is across the boat.

As the sails flap and cross the boat the helmsman changes sides facing aft and the crew releases the jib.

5.6 Tacking – aft mainsheet.

Helmsman calls 'lee oh' and pushes helm away. Her aft foot is across the boat. As the sails flap and come across, she swivels the tiller extension ahead of her as she crouches across the boat facing forwards.

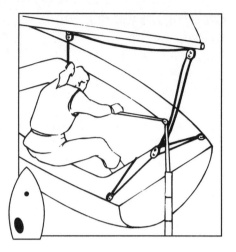

Initially, the helmsman steers with the forward hand grasping the tiller extension from behind her back.

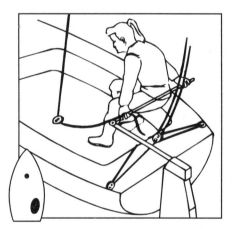

Once steady on the new course, she swaps hands and brings the tiller extension back in front of her in the usual 'dagger grip'.

5.7 Tacking – centre mainsheet.

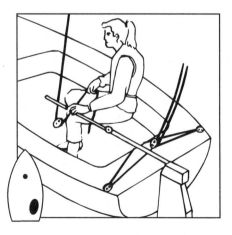

Centre mainsheet tacking

When tacking in a boat with centre mainsheet the main difference is that the person at the helm has the mainsheet forward and so faces forward through the tack. There is no need to change hands before tacking but this should be done after the tack as shown in figure 5.7. The helmsman checks that the intended new course will take them clear of any obstructions or other boats and calls 'ready about'. The crew also checks for obstructions and if clear replies 'ready'. The crew's actions are the same as with an aft mainsheet boat.

Getting out of irons

A frequent problem when tacking is that if the manoeuvre is attempted with insufficient boat speed or not enough centreboard, if the tiller is central too soon or the crew sheets the jib in on the new side too soon, the boat can stall, pointing head to wind in the *no go zone*. This is when the boat is pointing closer than about 45 degrees to the *true wind* (see figure 3.7).

5.8 Backing the jib to get out of irons.

The sails will be flapping, producing no drive and the rudder will at first do nothing to help as it is sitting dead in the water. This position is said to be 'in irons'. It is fairly simple to get out of by having the crew grab a jib sheet close to the sail and hold it out to one side. This will make the wind blow into the 'wrong' side of it and is called *backing the jib*. If it is important which way the boat turns, say to *port* then the jib should be backed on the opposite side (to *starboard* here). It will have the effect of blowing the bow of the boat away from the wind and you will turn on to a point with the wind blowing across the side of the boat. Then the crew can let go and you will be *lying to* ready to start sailing again.

Sailing upwind

So far we have sailed across the wind on a reach and made some alterations to our course but we have only really made progress across the wind and come back again. The next *point of sailing* to learn is when we want to make progress to a point which lies upwind of our starting point. As we saw in Chapter 3 we cannot sail directly upwind so if we want to make progress upwind we have to zigzag our way there. This is called *beating*. We have already made shallow tacks across the wind but now we must learn how to sail as efficiently as we can upwind on each leg. This is sailing close hauled – sailing close to the wind with the sheets hauled in tight. It is important that we do not try to sail too close to the wind otherwise the boat will keep stalling in the no go zone. The opposite of this is if we bear away from the wind too far in which case the boat does not make such good progress to windward. Sailing upwind well is one of the crucial skills of the sailor and takes lots of practice to do well.

Start by sailing on a beam reach with the sails trimmed correctly, the boat balanced and the centreboard about half-way down. Then luff up a little so you are sailing closer to the wind on a close reach. You should have trimmed the sails by sheeting them in and lowered the centreboard more. You will also have had to shift your combined weight more to windward to counteract the extra heeling forces. As you sail closer to the wind these actions have to be repeated but there comes a stage when the sails are sheeted in about as far as they will go, the centreboard is fully down and if you luff up any more you will be into the no go zone and the boat will stall. To check that you are sailing close hauled along the edge of the no go zone you can make a very slight course alteration to windward to see what happens.

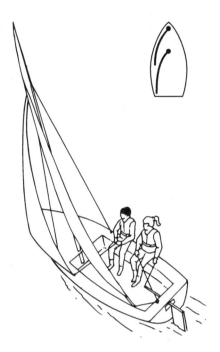

Mainsail sheeted in fairly hard, can be eased in gusts. Jib sheeted in hard, telltales streaming aft. Centreboard lowered fully to maximize leeway. Boat trim and balance: helmsman and crew weight slightly forward and to windward. Tiller movements small and steady. The helmsman can luff up a little in gusts. Keep a good lookout as the course made good will take you into the obscured area behind the jib.

5.9 Sailing close hauled.

You know from sail trimming that when you sheet out the sails just a little too far then the luff starts to lift and then flap and you must sheet in again to present the sail to the wind at the optimum angle. When you sail close hauled the same thing is happening. You are still trying to present the sails to the wind at the optimum angle but you do so by leaving them sheeted in while the whole boat changes course. If you luff up a little too far the luff of the sails should lift or begin to flap. You cannot sheet in any more so you bear away just enough to fill the sails again. If you sail even closer to the wind the signs are fairly obvious: the sails start to shake and if you did nothing about it the boat would stop in irons. Letting it reach this stage is rather inefficient though so as you become more proficient try and sense the earlier stages of steering into the no go zone. The windward jib telltales lifting, the jib luff not quite filling properly, the boat heeling less and slowing down, in a steady wind all these things happen before the jib starts to really flap.

The other concern when sailing close hauled is to stay close to the wind and not let the boat bear away too far. The signs of this are less immediately obvious and so this is a common mistake of the beginner.

You can use the burgee or your head and ears to keep checking on the wind direction to make sure you are not bearing away towards a beam reach. Also you can check that you are close hauled by occasionally luffing up very slightly. The early signs of steering into the no go zone should become apparent, if they do not you can luff up again until you are close hauled. If you do bear away too far then the signs are those of having the sails sheeted in too tight for the course you are on: the leeward jib telltales lift, the boat heels more and although it will continue to sail it will be going slower.

Sailing downwind

Sailing downwind is often considered to be the most relaxing point of sailing as sail trim is less critical, heeling and leeway are minimal and the boat's motion is usually easier. It is still important to pay close attention though if you want to get the best from the boat.

If you have room to do so spend some time beating upwind to give you an area you can sail back down to practise your downwind technique. This is usually better than sailing downwind of your start point as it might be difficult to judge how long it will take to return upwind.

Start from a beam reach again and bear away until the wind is coming from diagonally behind you (this is now a *broad reach*). It is important to sheet out the mainsail as you bear away, so that the steering effect of the sail is not working against the rudder and making it harder to turn. The centreboard should now be about three-quarters raised. If your boat has a daggerboard be careful not to raise it to a height where it would be caught by the boom or the kicking strap. The helmsman and crew shift their weight slightly further aft to keep the boat trim correct.

It is best at first to concentrate your downwind sailing on broad reaching effectively. It is possible to sail the boat directly downwind on a *dead run* but this takes more practice and getting it wrong can cause you to involuntarily turn the boat through the wind bringing the boom across the boat – an accidental *gybe* which is well worth avoiding.

At times on your broad reach you may have found the jib collapsing with no wind in it as it gets in the lee of the mainsail. This happens when you bear away a little further than a broad reach and is the sign that you are on a *training run*. It is worth practising finding this point of sailing as it is a good point from which to make a controlled gybe. The jib should lie slack and the jib sheets hang fairly loose. If the jib starts to cross to the windward side of the boat then you have come even further downwind and must luff slightly to come back on to a training run.

5.10 Broad reach.

Mainsail sheet out when bearing away and then trimmed if necessary. Do not sheet the jib in tight to keep it 'tidy'. If it gets in the lee of the mainsail and starts to collapse, luff up slightly until it fills with wind again. Centreboard about three-quarters raised. Helmsman and crew weight is to aft to keep boat on level trim. The crew may be sitting to leeward to keep boat level.

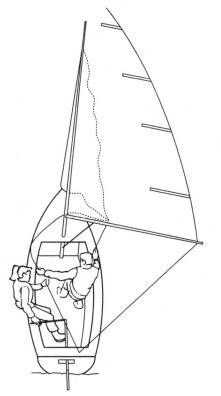

Mainsail is fully sheeted out against the leeward shroud. Jib is lying slack with sheets hanging loose. Centreboard is raised nearly all the way. The helmsman sits to windward to keep a view of sails and course. The crew sits to leeward and in light winds may need to hold the boom out. Kicking strap should be adjusted to prevent boom from lifting which could result in an accidental gybe.

5.11 Training run.

Gybing

So far whenever you have changed course so that the wind has changed from one side of the boat to the other then you have done so by bringing the bow of the boat through the wind – tacking. You will remember that at the mid-point the bow was pointing directly into the wind in the no go zone with the sails flapping. We shall now look at the manoeuvre when the boat is brought through the wind when going downwind. This is called a gybe and at the mid-point the bow is pointing directly away from the wind. In a gybe the mainsail moves quickly from one side to the other and from having wind in it on one side immediately fills with wind on the other side as it crosses the boat. This means that it travels with considerable power in strong winds and as the boom has a fair way to travel it can hit you hard if you get in the way! It is particularly important with gybing to practise first in lighter winds. It is also a good idea to make the sail less powerful by *reefing* it if you can (see Chapter 6).

The best point from which to gybe is a training run as described above. It is important to be aware of the course and to hold a steady training run until you actually intend to start the gybe. A common error is to lose concentration on steering as you sort out the preparation for gybing which can result in it all happening rather sooner than intended. For this reason make sure you can confidently hold a training run before you attempt a gybe (you can give yourself a bit more room for error by gybing from a broad reach).

Aft mainsheet gybing

When helming, check the mainsheet is not in a tangle, check the area you are going to sail into and call 'stand by to gybe'. The crew checks the centreboard is nearly all the way up (or the daggerboard is not too high for the boom), also checks the area you are sailing into and replies 'yes'. Figure 5.12 shows the next course of events.

Centre mainsheet gybing

The main difference between gybing with aft and centre mainsheet dinghies is that with the latter the helmsman faces forwards throughout the manoeuvre and does not change hands on the tiller extension and mainsheet until after the gybe is complete. The helmsman checks the mainsheet and the area they are going to sail into and calls 'stand by to gybe'. The crew checks the centreboard is nearly all the way up (or the daggerboard is not too high for the boom), also checks the

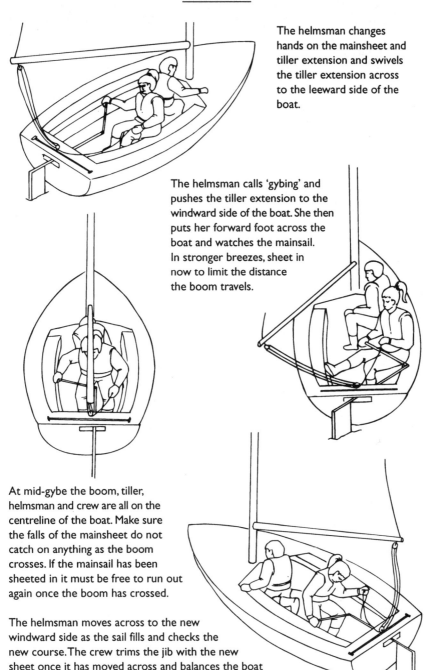

The helmsman changes hands on the mainsheet and tiller extension and swivels the tiller extension across to the leeward side of the boat.

The helmsman calls 'gybing' and pushes the tiller extension to the windward side of the boat. She then puts her forward foot across the boat and watches the mainsail. In stronger breezes, sheet in now to limit the distance the boom travels.

At mid-gybe the boom, tiller, helmsman and crew are all on the centreline of the boat. Make sure the falls of the mainsheet do not catch on anything as the boom crosses. If the mainsail has been sheeted in it must be free to run out again once the boom has crossed.

The helmsman moves across to the new windward side as the sail fills and checks the new course. The crew trims the jib with the new sheet once it has moved across and balances the boat for the new course.

5.12 Gybing – aft mainsheet.

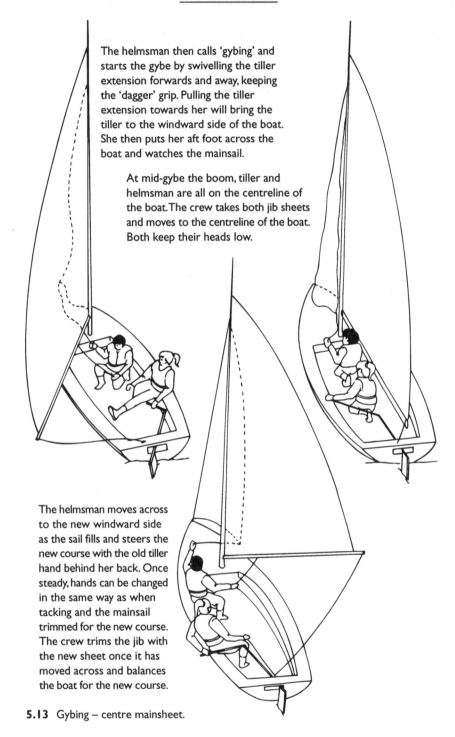

The helmsman then calls 'gybing' and starts the gybe by swivelling the tiller extension forwards and away, keeping the 'dagger' grip. Pulling the tiller extension towards her will bring the tiller to the windward side of the boat. She then puts her aft foot across the boat and watches the mainsail.

At mid-gybe the boom, tiller and helmsman are all on the centreline of the boat. The crew takes both jib sheets and moves to the centreline of the boat. Both keep their heads low.

The helmsman moves across to the new windward side as the sail fills and steers the new course with the old tiller hand behind her back. Once steady, hands can be changed in the same way as when tacking and the mainsail trimmed for the new course. The crew trims the jib with the new sheet once it has moved across and balances the boat for the new course.

5.13 Gybing – centre mainsheet.

area they are sailing into and replies 'yes'. Figure 5.13 shows the next course of events.

Gybing problems and refinements

A common occurrence after a bad gybe is when the boat turns up towards the wind and the boat heels over alarmingly. This is called a *broach* and can easily result in a capsize.

Factors which can cause or compound a broach:

- The mainsheet gets caught and is therefore effectively sheeted in tight once it fills with wind on the new side. This causes excessive heeling which in turn makes the boat turn even further to windward.
- The tiller was not centred soon enough causing the boat to turn much more than planned. This is the most common cause of gybing problems.
- The weight of helmsman and crew might not have been moved at the right time to balance the boat effectively and keep it level.
- The centreboard may have been down too far causing the wind to have greater heeling force.

If you are suffering a broach and looking at an impending capsize then quick action to remedy the first three of these points might keep you dry.

Quick action to avoid a capsize:

- Free the mainsheet from whatever might have obstructed it. (In future sheeting in as you gybe can help by leaving less slack in the system to get caught. It is then sheeted out again as the sail fills on the new side and letting it run through the mainsheet block provides an effective shock absorber. The sheet must be free to run out through the block though otherwise you just create the same problem by different means.)
- Sit out on the new windward side and pull the tiller towards you to bear away from the wind.
- Use crew weight to help keep the boat level.
- Check the centreboard position for the new point of sailing.

The dead run – sailing exactly downwind

I have purposely left this point of sailing until last as it ought to be avoided until you can hold a training run knowing which way to move the tiller without thinking too much, and gybe confidently in control. The reason for this is that sailing on a dead run is a very specific course with little room for variation. If you put the tiller the wrong way you will gybe almost immediately so you need to be used to the signs that tell you how you are doing in relation to the wind.

Find an area that gives you plenty of room downwind, preferably as before by sailing upwind first. Start from a beam reach again and bear away to a broad reach and then a training run. Watch the jib falling slack and bear away a small amount further. The jib should start to come across to windward but watch the back edge (leech) of the main-sail as well. You are trying to get the jib to set happily on the wind-ward side. If the jib falls back to leeward then you bear away a little to bring it back. If the mainsail leech starts to collapse the mainsail is close to gybing across the boat so you luff up slightly to keep it where it is. Sailing with the sails set on each side like this is called *running goose-winged*.

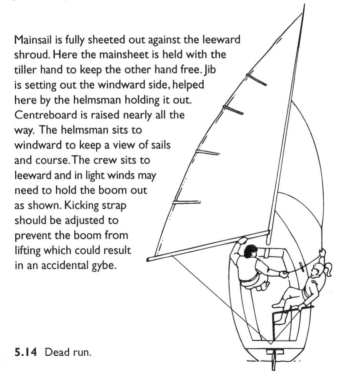

Mainsail is fully sheeted out against the leeward shroud. Here the mainsheet is held with the tiller hand to keep the other hand free. Jib is setting out the windward side, helped here by the helmsman holding it out. Centreboard is raised nearly all the way. The helmsman sits to windward to keep a view of sails and course. The crew sits to leeward and in light winds may need to hold the boom out as shown. Kicking strap should be adjusted to prevent the boom from lifting which could result in an accidental gybe.

5.14 Dead run.

The essentials

You will see by now that it is necessary for helmsman and crew to make constant adjustments as the boat sails around a course. Even as you sail in a straight line you may think you have got a nice long reach to relax on but small changes of wind, either in direction or speed affect the boat and need to be acted on. You also need to be aware of where the boat is travelling to. Remember in Chapter 3 how the boat makes leeway, the sideways movement through the water resisted by the centreboard? The boat is pointing in one direction (your *heading*) but may be travelling in a slightly different direction. We call this direction of travel *course made good*. In tidal situations this is even further from your heading (see Chapter 8).

Whilst you are sailing you should be paying constant attention to the 'five essentials' of sail trim, centreboard position, balance, boat trim and course made good. Whenever anything changes all these factors should be considered and re-adjusted as necessary.

A good way of putting all this into practice is to sail circles around an imaginary course. Think carefully about these 'five essentials' at each stage and at first choose a large empty area to sail around. Concentrate on getting things right at each stage and as you gain more confidence make the circles gradually smaller. Once you have things under control you can manoeuvre around free mooring buoys or other markers but do not risk going too close and bumping into obstructions – give them all a wide berth.

6

Going ashore

Slow manoeuvring in slack water

A major consideration when returning ashore is to slow down sufficiently so as not to pile yourself, boat and crew into a solid object at a
rate of knots. The various available obstructions can be pontoons, other
boats, harbour walls, jetties and the beach itself. All methods of going
ashore therefore require a careful approach well in control of your
speed.

We have seen that on a beam reach we can slow the boat down by
letting the sails out to flap, so removing the drive, and the boat will
come to rest in the lying-to position. It does this more happily with the
wind slightly forward of abeam – (with the boat on a *fine reach*). With
the wind abeam the mainsail will be at the limit of its freedom to be
sheeted out and therefore spill wind.

If the wind is abaft (aft of) the beam (on a broad reach for example) then the mainsail can be let out against the leeward shroud but
cannot go far enough to spill wind. You cannot slow to a stop on this
point of sailing. The principle here is that of being in a position to sig-
nificantly slow the boat down. With the wind behind us we can slow
the boat down by sheeting in the mainsail to sail less efficiently, or
even by dragging something through the water astern but we cannot
stop completely. For this it is crucial that we must be able to spill
wind.

We also want to be able to have as much manoeuvrability as possible. We know that we can spill wind when the boat is close hauled for
instance but this point of sailing is not flexible as we cannot turn to
windward and still keep the boat driving (we would be in the no go
zone). For these reasons sailing on a fine reach is the favoured line of
approach in many situations.

In a current or *tidal stream* we sometimes slow down by heading into
the stream but downwind. This has to be done under jib alone and is
described below in tidal moorings and in Chapter 8.

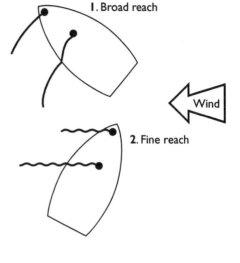

1. Broad reach

1. Sailing on a broad reach the mainsheet is slack but the boom and the mainsail are up against the shroud and producing drive.

Wind

2. Fine reach

2. On a fine reach the helmsman can slow down by sheeting out (to spill), speed up by sheeting in (to fill), and change course in either direction.

6.1 Manoeuvring on a fine reach.

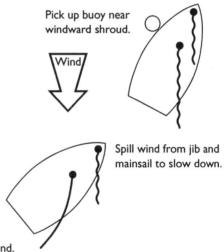

Pick up buoy near windward shroud.

Wind

Spill wind from jib and mainsail to slow down.

6.2 Approaching a mooring head to wind.

Returning to a mooring in slack water

Your boat may be kept on a mooring or you may want to pick one up for a short stop. Prepare the *painter* or a line to *make fast* with. Approach on a close reach allowing for leeway and sheet out the jib so it flaps. Slow down more by spilling the mainsail, bringing the boat to a halt with the buoy near the windward shroud. Make fast the mooring line, lower the sails, raise the centreboard and remove the rudder.

Returning to a mooring in a tidal stream or current

Once the water is moving under you things become a little more difficult so first read the relevant sections of Chapter 8, particularly referring
to the use of *transits* to judge your *course made good*. It is also important
to check which way any tide is running so you can approach using the
appropriate technique.

For returning to a mooring in a tideway when the wind is in about
the same direction as the tide the above method also holds good
although clearly you need to make allowance for the strength of the tide.

If the tide is running against the wind however then it is important to
approach the mooring from downtide so the boat will stop when you
get there. On this occasion it is necessary to slow down while sailing
downwind, which is done under jib alone. This is because only the jib
can spill wind with the wind behind you. Sail upwind of the buoy, prepare the painter or line to make fast with, luff up and drop the mainsail.
Then raise the centreboard and sail downwind under jib alone. Sheet out
the jib to slow down and let it fly completely when you reach the buoy
and make fast. Finally lower the jib and remove the rudder.

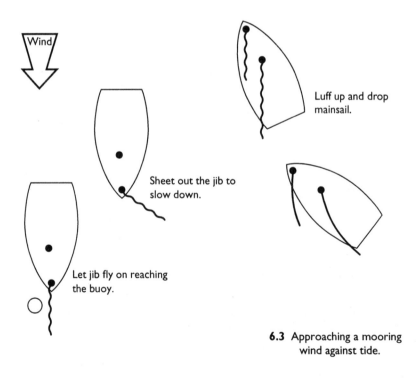

Wind

Luff up and drop
mainsail.

Sheet out the jib to
slow down.

Let jib fly on reaching
the buoy.

6.3 Approaching a mooring
wind against tide.

Returning to a beach
Wind along the shore

As with sailing off this is probably the easiest scenario. Approach on a fine reach raising the centreboard and rudder as necessary as you sail into shallow water. Bear in mind that when you do this the boat will make more leeway. Slow down by letting the sheets out as you near the beach, finally turning head to wind as the crew jumps out and holds the bow.

Wind blowing offshore

You will need to keep the centreboard lowered to beat into the shore but obviously you also need to raise it as you reach shallow water. Make sure you raise it in good time, particularly if you have a daggerboard which, as it does not swivel up, is more likely to break if it touches.

Wind blowing onshore

Care needs to be taken here to approach safely as otherwise it would be easy to ram the boat into the shore. The easiest way to approach is to find a clear patch of water not far from the beach, turn up into the wind and lower the mainsail. You then come in under jib alone able to spill wind to slow down if necessary and have the crew ready to jump out in the shallows to catch the boat and stop it if necessary.

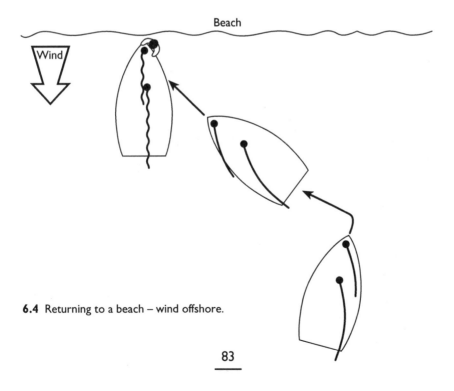

6.4 Returning to a beach – wind offshore.

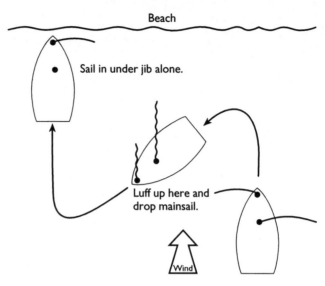

6.5 Returning to a beach – wind onshore.

Returning to a pontoon

With a pontoon it is likely that you have less of a target than the beach so the approach will need to be more precise.

Whenever possible it is best in non-tidal situations to approach so that you end up head to wind with sails flapping. Bear in mind throughout which way you will sail if things go disastrously wrong! As with any manoeuvre it is worth planning what you are trying to do and make sure you and the crew are well prepared. You may need fenders to protect the boat and you will need a painter or warps to tie it up. It is much better to get all this sorted out in advance than be making your final 'controlled approach' with your head in a locker rooting about for a bit of string.

You should also tell your crew where you are planning to go and what you expect them to do. Do not be afraid to take firm charge either as chaos can reign if no one knows what is happening. On the Outward Bound cutters we will try to teach a team of eight or more to work together effectively and this usually happens with strong leadership. Some processes can be worked out with long committee meetings but if the boat is rapidly heading for the harbour wall with six people pulling on oars and warps and fenders yet to be prepared then it is the commanding skipper who will sort it out best. The example from larger boats is relevant to the dinghy sailor even though the task may be simple with only one other person involved. I get a satisfaction from

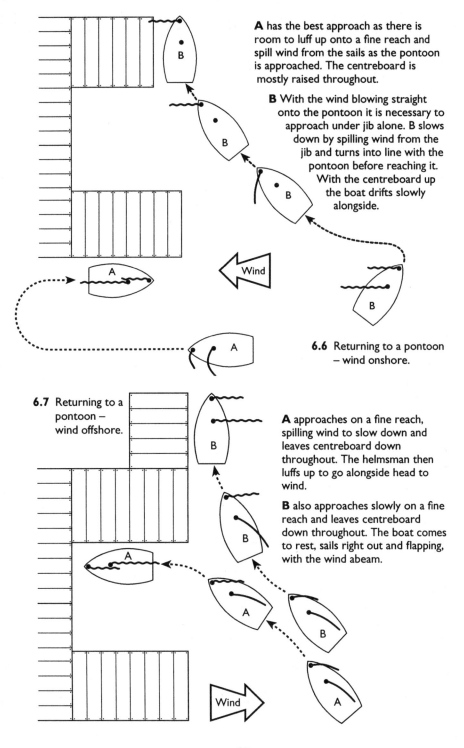

A has the best approach as there is room to luff up onto a fine reach and spill wind from the sails as the pontoon is approached. The centreboard is mostly raised throughout.

B With the wind blowing straight onto the pontoon it is necessary to approach under jib alone. B slows down by spilling wind from the jib and turns into line with the pontoon before reaching it. With the centreboard up the boat drifts slowly alongside.

Wind

6.6 Returning to a pontoon – wind onshore.

6.7 Returning to a pontoon – wind offshore.

A approaches on a fine reach, spilling wind to slow down and leaves centreboard down throughout. The helmsman then luffs up to go alongside head to wind.

B also approaches slowly on a fine reach and leaves centreboard down throughout. The boat comes to rest, sails right out and flapping, with the wind abeam.

Wind

handling a small boat well, just as I do with a larger vessel but if things go wrong it is the skipper who must accept the blame.

I managed to bump headlong into the harbour wall today. It wasn't long after I had been complimented by a local boatman on how handy my little sailing boat was in the way it dodged around in the harbour. I smugly thought to myself 'well it depends how you handle her of course' and replied 'Yes, for a heavy dinghy she's pretty manoeuvrable really'. That was before I suffered the complication of getting other people aboard. I always thought that the big boat skippering style had no place in relaxed dinghy day-sailing. Not any more. There were four of us aboard, I pushed off and we ghosted along. I was not in a hurry to get out of the harbour and thought drifting around would give plenty of time to get things stowed properly. The outboard was not working and Uncle Bert reckoned there could not be that much to go wrong with a little, three-horsepower, two-stroke engine and busied himself with it. He obviously enjoys that sort of thing and he is pretty good with car engines so I left him to it and showed my father how to tidy and stow the halyards, warps and fenders.

Shortly afterwards we were in the middle of one of those interminable tacks in wispy airs and pointing directly towards the harbour wall just a few feet off. I had decided it was time to get the oars out and find some wind when suddenly the outboard shocked us all as it temporarily burst into life showing more eagerness than it has done all season. The worst thing was that I had even thought 'I'd rather Uncle Bert stopped pulling on it just here'. It was obvious what would happen if it started but I didn't want to seem too bossy on a holiday weekend. I am not sure that I even told him that it is always in gear and I obviously had not told him what to do if it started. I was torn between rushing to the bow to fend off or rushing to the stern to steer us away. It was too late to do either though as the engine drove us straight into the wall. Fortunately no damage was done but needless to say the outboard did not keep going long enough to see us into clear wind!

As you come alongside do not forget to keep the boat balanced. Only one person needs to grasp the pontoon and can either take a line ashore or can step off and hold the boat by the shroud. Once you are safely alongside tie the boat up with bow and stern lines and make sure the fenders are doing the job. Drop the sails and secure them, raise the centreboard and remove rudder and tiller.

Recovering on to a trailer

If you launched the boat from a trolley you should not have too much trouble putting it back on again. Whatever you did with the sails to launch do the same in reverse now unless the wind has changed. Get the submerged trolley under the boat and pull them both up the slipway until the hull is touching the trolley. Double check at this stage that the dinghy is sitting centrally on the trolley and if so attach the painter to the trolley. Then haul the dinghy up the slipway using as many people as you can. If it is a light-weight single-hander then two people is plenty but with heavier dinghies the more the merrier. Finally, as you de-rig the boat keep an eye out for other people you can give a hand to.

Bar stool learning

Think back over the sail you have had and see if you can recall the highlights. This need not happen in the bar of course but the clubhouse post mortem is always good fun. There is a serious side to it as well of course and although everyone tends to be a bit self-critical at times, taken in the right way this can be beneficial. If one or two things with your sail did not go entirely according to plan then make a note of what went wrong. It is quite likely of course that you have not the faintest idea what went wrong, in which case remember at least what you were trying to do so that you can ask advice and work on it next time. Similarly if it went like a dream then do not just pat yourself on the back, work out why so you can repeat it next time. What did you perhaps avoid trying because you felt it was a bit beyond your ability? Do you have a goal for something you want to achieve next time? What might help you work towards it?

If you have come to sailing through an Outward Bound course then you will have experienced the value of asking these sorts of questions of yourself. Reviewing your progress will really help when it comes to learning anything effectively so amidst the fun and hilarity that I hope you have sailing, take a little time to give some thought to your learning and strive always to improve.

7

Further skills

So far you have learnt how to take a boat for a sail and manoeuvre around in any direction but there is yet more to learn before you could be considered proficient. This chapter adds more of the important basic skills which you need to learn, such as capsize recovery, reefing, anchoring and more on balance, and then looks at how you can improve the skills you have already learnt with a bit more attention to detail. I assume that you have the use of a reasonably well set up, basic boat but do not go as far as describing some advanced skills that require equipment not covered by this book. The excitement of sailing fast using spinnaker and trapeze is something that is best experienced with some further practical instruction when you are ready, and can be backed up then by further reading.

Heaving to

In Chapter 5 we looked at the lying-to position as a way of temporarily stopping the boat with the sails flapping. *Heaving to* is a more refined version of this which makes the boat lie more quietly and balanced. It is an excellent position to take up in order to sort out a problem, reef the sails, pour a cup of tea or do anything else which would otherwise be rather difficult with the boat careering along demanding your full attention.

Figure 7.1 shows a dinghy hove to on the *port tack*. When you heave to you need to be aware that the boat will drift downwind and a little forward so you need to keep your eyes on what is happening around you. When choosing a tack on which to heave to, the consideration of having plenty of sea room comes first. If then there is still a choice choose a *starboard tack* so you will have right of way over other sailing boats (see collision regulations in Chapter 9).

The easiest way to heave to is to tack the boat but leave the jib sheet cleated where it was. The jib is now backed. This makes the boat bear away from the wind so the tiller is pushed to leeward to counteract that. The mainsheet is eased right out so it has no drive but with just

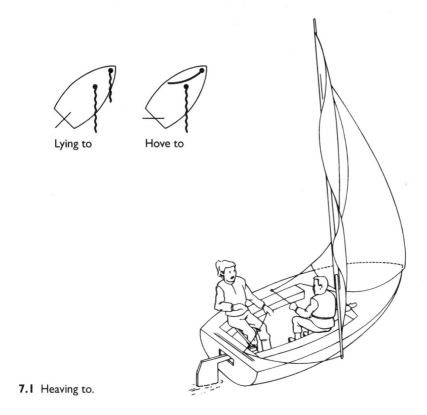

Lying to   Hove to

7.1 Heaving to.

enough mainsheet tension to stop the sail flapping wildly. Raising the centreboard a little reduces your heeling and will make it easier to balance the boat. Once the boat has come to rest then the tiller can be wedged or lashed to leeward.

The boat should now sit quite happily and look after itself. The backed jib tries to make the bow turn away from the wind but as soon as it does the mainsail gains some drive and moves the boat forward through the water. Once the boat is moving forwards the rudder starts to work and the boat luffs up again. This in turn spills any wind from the mainsail and with the jib backed the boat will not gain enough speed to tack and will stop in the water. Some boats jog up and down quite happily like this while others will sit steady with the same attitude to the wind. Experiment with fine adjustments to mainsheet and centreboard positions and be aware of boat trim to get best results.

When you want to start sailing again just straighten the tiller, sheet the jib across to leeward and sheet in the mainsail.

Boat balance and handling

In Chapter 5 there was frequent reference to boat balance and the use of combined weight of helmsman and crew to keep the boat sailing as level as possible. This indeed is generally the case particularly if we want the boat to plane. Planing is when the boat lifts up on to its own bow wave and skims along the surface of the water. This is encouraged by sitting a little further aft than usual and requires very gentle use of the tiller as the *helm* becomes very light and responsive to the slightest movement.

Sometimes however it is useful to make the boat heel one way or the other so this section aims to get you thinking more about boat balance as something you actively adjust to work for you rather than react to in order to stay dry. Work on an understanding with your crew that leads you to correct balance smoothly. You should get to know who makes the first moves to adjust the balance so you are not both adjusting but working in smooth harmony. This can only come with lots of practice and eventually the feel for the boat will become instinctive.

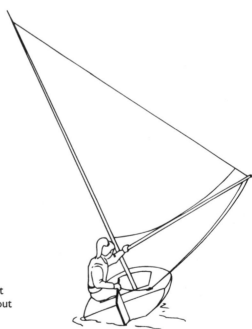

The helmsman can heel the boat to windward but in light winds must hold the boom out to stop it swinging down.

7.2 Single-hander on a run.

Hulls designed to plane will do so best with the boat level. That is fine but what about when they are not planing? The planing hull has a large area of flat underbody aft which causes a lot of resistance due to friction when moving through the water. When these boats are not planing then they will sail a little better by lifting some of that area out of the water by heeling. This is called reducing the wetted surface area. Non-planing hulls also usually have less wetted surface area when heeled slightly so they benefit in light airs from having a little heel induced.

Heeling the boat a little to leeward in light airs also improves sail efficiency when reaching and sailing upwind. Gravity helps the sails adopt a smooth curve when there would not be enough wind to fill them properly when upright.

Heeling to windward looks unnatural but is in fact used by single-handers on a run. The effort concentrated on that one sail can be a long way from the centreline of the boat when it is sheeted a long way out. Heeling to windward helps by bringing the centre of effort more over the boat and improves handling. Beware of sheeting out too far though because if the sail is set too far forward the heeling effort will be to windward and you will quickly capsize.

More on steering

Heeling is also an important way of helping to steer the boat. The best sailors use all the forces acting on the boat to help with steering and do not rely on the rudder to overpower the other forces of heeling and sail balance described in figure 7.3 and 7.4.

To bring this together try a little experiment in light winds. Sail on a fine reach and then sheet in the mainsail. This should, if nothing else changes, turn you to windward. On this occasion though, correct that with the tiller so that you maintain the previous course with the sail sheeted in too tight. This causes more heel to leeward which also tries to turn you to windward. With two forces trying to turn you to windward, see what happens if you gently use just the tiller to bear away. I say gently and in light winds because setting these forces against each other puts unfair stress on your rudder if you are heavy handed. You will learn to recognize the feel given here of the boat resisting the turn downwind.

Now go back to the fine reach but trimmed correctly. This time let the mainsheet fly and see how easy it is to bear away. The boat will have come upright when you sheeted out and as you will have been sitting out a little it may even have heeled to windward. This will have helped the turn along with the sheeted in jib and the free mainsail. A smaller amount of tiller movement will have been necessary.

This 'experiment' shows the benefits of using the forces in harmony. Think of the boat as pivoting around the sails and using them as you turn, not trimming them afterwards. Use heeling as well and your rudder movement will be smaller and smoother. Whenever the rudder is turned away from the centreline of the boat it slows you down to some degree. Using the rudder less you will not only turn quicker but travel faster as well. In the example above your body weight was working for you without you really positively shifting it. By using heeling as well you will soon see that you do not even need the rudder.

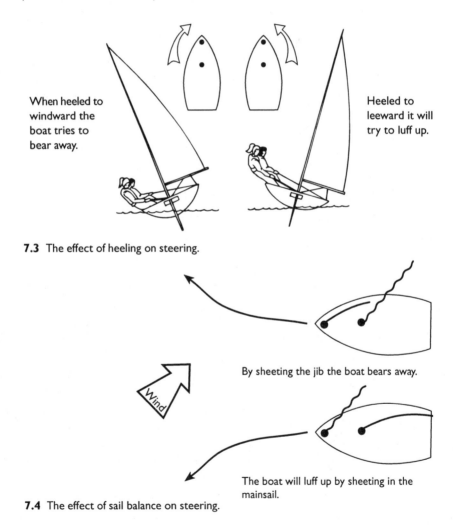

When heeled to windward the boat tries to bear away.

Heeled to leeward it will try to luff up.

7.3 The effect of heeling on steering.

By sheeting the jib the boat bears away.

Wind

The boat will luff up by sheeting in the mainsail.

7.4 The effect of sail balance on steering.

Rudderless sailing

It sounds difficult but you have already shown how much you can do without it so try taking it off altogether. You will need plenty of room as you may quickly lose control of the boat while you are getting used to the technique. Choose a time with light winds and sail to a good clear stretch of water and stop the boat by lying to. Take the rudder off the transom and lay it in the bottom of the boat keeping it tied on to something. Now just go sailing using heeling and sail balance to steer a course. If you have two people on board it is best for just one person to operate the *sheets* and balance the boat, the other sitting still. At first your course will seem rather erratic but as you get the hang of it things will get smoother and you should be able to steer a course quite successfully.

In my heavy cruising dinghy I was once tidying away fenders and warps that my friend had not quite put away to my rather exact requirements. Teasing me as I probably deserved he asked how I managed to stow warps and fenders so neatly when I was on my own. At risk of making him feel superfluous I showed him by taking him off the tiller, lashing it, and cleating off the mainsheet. We proceeded a short way like this while I finished making things shipshape, steering by shifting my weight in the boat. Fortunately he forgave my showing off and we then had great fun seeing what ridiculously contrived courses we could sail without the rudder.

Setting the sail to suit the conditions
Adjusting the sail shape

In Chapter 4 I mentioned that a taut luff is important for sailing close to the wind. I also touched on how the mainsail clew outhaul can be adjusted to flatten the mainsail in stronger winds. If you want a 'rule of thumb' then pull everything in tight on a beat and let things off a bit when reaching and running. Another good general rule is to look at the curve of the sail and check whether any creases or strange shapes are disturbing the airflow. Let us look at sail controls now in more detail.

The *jib halyard* can usually be set up as tight as possible and stay that way. A slack jib halyard creates awful curves between the hanks.

Jib sheet fairleads. On some boats these can be moved, changing the angle of pull on the jib. Generally speaking you bring them inboard and forward when close hauled. This helps the sail take up a good shape in relation to the mainsail – (a parallel 'slot' between the two sails increases the airflow and improves sail efficiency). As you sail further off the wind they move progressively outboard and a little aft.

Mainsail luff tension is best if easily adjustable and so is usually controlled by a cunningham (see page 48) with the main halyard having been set up and left. A taut luff brings the fullness of the sail forward which is best when sailing close hauled. This needs to be eased off as you bear away from the wind.

Mainsail shape can be further adjusted by the outhaul and kicking strap. The outhaul should be set up tight for windy conditions but can be eased off in lighter winds and when reaching and running.

The kicking strap in a simple way works to stop the boom from lifting and therefore the top of the sail twisting off downwind. This would cause wind to spill from the top of the sail which is less efficient and can cause the boat to be unstable going downwind. Powerful kicking straps can also bend the mast by pushing the boom forward. This works to flatten the sail and controls the shape of the back edge (leech). It is adjusted frequently to suit each point of sailing. Upwind it is tensioned to pull in the top of the leech and in strong winds pulled in hard to flatten the sail. While reaching and running it is eased giving more shape to the sail. Remember to avoid allowing the boom to lift while running though.

If you have a *mainsheet traveller* then use it with the mainsheet to control the mainsail twist. Moving it to leeward helps flatten the sail by putting the mainsheet block under the boom. In light winds allow the mainsail to adopt a better twist by leaving the traveller centrally positioned or even moving it up to windward a little.

Reefing

In stronger winds using the above controls to flatten and depower the sail will only work to a certain degree. There comes a time when in order to stay upright you have to spill wind by luffing or easing out the mainsheet. This is fine for the odd gust when you need full sail to get the most of the average wind but if you find yourself spilling wind a lot then, in many boats, you can shorten the sail by reefing it. As you gain experience you will be able to judge better from ashore what sail area would be suitable for the wind you expect. It is much better at first to put a reef in ashore than to go out and feel things are a bit out of control. When learning it is a good idea to reef the boat in all but the lightest of winds so that everything happens more slowly and calmly. This is a much better learning environment than the stress and possible chaos caused by feeling things are not in your control.

Reefing systems vary but I will describe three basic types here.

Roller reefing

Here the sail is reduced in size by rolling it around the boom.

Steps to roller reefing:

- Remove kicking strap and make sure mainsheet is slack.
- Have the sail hoisted by about two-thirds and temporarily make fast the halyard.
- Remove any sail battens in the section of sail you are rolling up.
- Then take a tuck in the aft edge (leech) of the sail. The aim of this is to finish with a boom that is level when the sail is hoisted again.
- Rotate the boom so the sail rolls around it, trapping the tuck you made. It is important to keep pulling back on the leech to make a smooth roll without creases. As this covers up the kicking strap attachment point it is necessary to roll a sail bag or reefing strop into the sail. This gives you something to attach the kicking strap to.
- Locate the boom back in the gooseneck and tension the halyard. You can then clip the kicking strap on to the sailbag or reefing strop and you are ready to go.

Slab reefing

Slab reefing involves securing the 'slab' of sail with strong eyes called cringles in luff and leech. These are held down by lines called *reefing pennants*. The dinghy in figure 7.6 is also equipped with a *topping lift* which supports the boom.

Reefing afloat

It is preferable to get the boat reefed down to the conditions while you are still ashore. Sometimes this may not have happened; perhaps you have misjudged the amount of wind you expected or maybe you are off for a few hours or a day sail and things have changed. Whatever the cause, you need to be able to put a reef in quickly and efficiently while you are afloat if the occasion arises. The longer the period you tend to go out sailing for, the more often you are likely to need to do this. For this reason boats that are well set up for cruising tend to be equipped with a topping lift (see figure 7.6) which makes the process easier.

Your first consideration will be where to put the boat while you put the reef in. On a mooring (or at anchor) is the best bet if it would keep the boat pointing into the wind and fixed in one place. Otherwise going hove to is the next easiest option. In this position the boat is

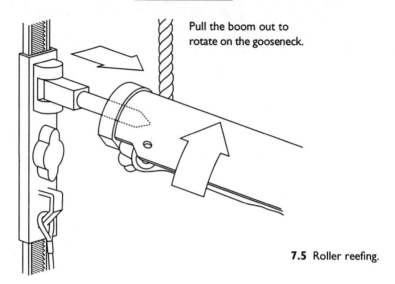

Pull the boom out to rotate on the gooseneck.

7.5 Roller reefing.

steady, the mainsail is free to flap and you are free to look after the job as the boat will look after itself. Obviously you need to choose a position where you have plenty of sea room and you need to keep a look out around you. The whole job should not take more than a couple of minutes so practise until you are slick at it.

Reefing single-handers

Sails that sleeve around the mast are not lowered to reef but are rolled around the mast. Not all single-handers are rigged this way but the popular Topper and Laser are. I recently sailed a 5m (16ft) ketch rigged this way and this technique also applied there.

Steps to reefing single-handers:

- Remove kicking strap, ease the outhaul right off, free the cunningham and if the boom fits on to a gooseneck then remove it.
- Rotate the mast, making sure you get tight, crease-free rolls of sail. If the sail is battened then this will limit the amount you can roll up without removing battens.
- Replace the boom and tension the cunningham.
- Tension the outhaul and kicking strap.

This is more difficult to achieve *under way* so it is preferable with these boats to get the sailplan right for the conditions before launching.

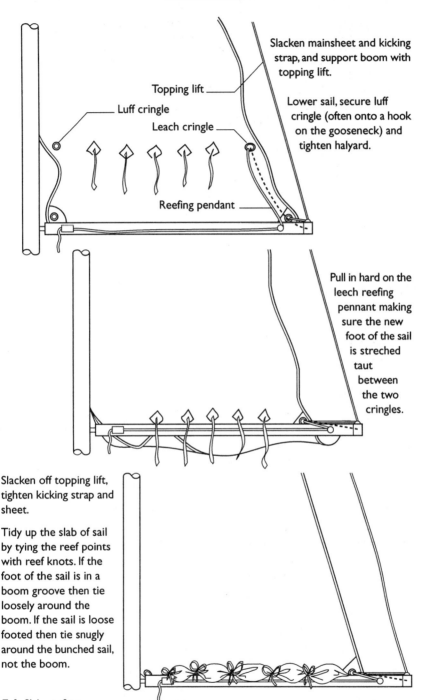

Slacken mainsheet and kicking strap, and support boom with topping lift.

Lower sail, secure luff cringle (often onto a hook on the gooseneck) and tighten halyard.

Topping lift

Luff cringle

Leach cringle

Reefing pendant

Pull in hard on the leech reefing pennant making sure the new foot of the sail is streched taut between the two cringles.

Slacken off topping lift, tighten kicking strap and sheet.

Tidy up the slab of sail by tying the reef points with reef knots. If the foot of the sail is in a boom groove then tie loosely around the boom. If the sail is loose footed then tie snugly around the bunched sail, not the boom.

7.6 Slab reefing.

Capsize recovery

Getting wet is definitely a part of dinghy sailing and capsizing should be considered an integral part of your training. In the conditions outlined as being sensible to start off in you might not capsize accidentally so you may need to make sure that you make it happen on purpose. It is important that you feel able to recover the boat with confidence and it is essential that you gain that confidence in conditions where it is a good bit of fun. Therefore it is best to practise when things are well in control and you have the cover of a safety boat. You do not want to be trying this for the first time in a force 4 or more when you might be sailing at the limit of your early ability. It should not be necessary to remind you to check the buoyancy but you will find out soon enough if there is a problem with it! Buoyancy bags should be full of air and strongly secured. Built in buoyancy tanks should be empty of water and often have a drain plug to check this.

Once the capsize has happened the first consideration is to stay with the boat. This should continue to be your priority even if for some reason you cannot right it. It has a large amount of buoyancy in it and will provide considerable support if necessary. It also presents a large target to spot and someone is likely to notice if you are in trouble. Read the section on indicating *distress* in Chapter 8, but if you just need a bit of a hand from the safety boat then a simple wave or whistle would be more appropriate. See figure 7.7 for actions to right the boat.

A boat full of water will be quite unstable so will have to be balanced carefully once upright. If the water level is near the top of the centreboard case then it is worth the crew doing a stint of baling before bringing the helmsman aboard. Modern dinghies tend to ship little water though and will self-bail once you get going again.

The crew helps the helmsman aboard at the windward shroud. This place is important as the wind will blow the mainsail to the leeward side, keeping the mainsheet out of the way and helping to balance the boat. If the helmsman is further aft then he or she will act as a drogue and the boat may blow around to head downwind. If this happened the sails would fill and off it would go and the helmsman would be dragged along, left behind or the boat would gybe accidently which might cause it to capsize again.

Once you are all aboard, sort out the mess, bale out if necessary and sail off when you are ready. Do not forget to keep an eye on your surroundings though. Once you are upright and the more empty you are, the quicker you will be drifting downwind. Do not waste time

Keep contact with the boat but avoid putting any weight on it. Both helmsman and crew swim to the stern and check that the other is OK. The helmsman checks the rudder and tiller are still in position. The crew frees the mainsheet and passes it to the helmsman.

Then the helmsman, holding on to the end of the mainsheet (to keep in touch with the boat), swims around the hull to the centreboard. The crew meanwhile swims to the top of the centreboard and lowers it without injuring the helmsman. You can talk to each other through the centreboard case.

The crew then frees the jibsheets and tosses the upper one over the boat to the helmsman.

The helmsman catches the jibsheet and leans back in the water with straight legs and feet against the lowest part of the hull possible. This should slowly start to right the boat.

It might be that the helmsman needs more leverage to right the boat and has to climb up on the centreboard. If you do this keep your weight at the hull end of the centreboard to avoid damage. Lean well back holding on to the jibsheet.

The crew can now lie in the water alongside the centreboard case supported by his buoyancy aid, still avoiding putting any weight on to the boat. As the boat comes upright the crew is scooped in.

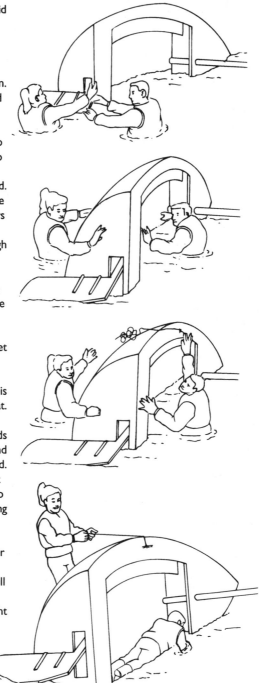

7.7 Capsize recovery.

emptying the boat out completely, as the self-bailers will drain the last of the water once you get moving quickly.

Windward capsize

If the boat capsizes to windward then the sail will end up lying in the water to windward. If the above procedure is followed then the wind is likely to get under the mainsail as soon as it lifts and as the boat rapidly rights itself with the crew weight on the leeward side a swift repeat capsize is extremely likely. To avoid this it is necessary to get the boat approximately head to wind before attempting to right it. This is best done by holding on to the bow and letting the hull swing down-wind of you. Righting can then proceed as outlined above.

Full inversion

Sometimes the boat will turn fully upside-down. This will take longer to sort out but is not usually too great a problem. The helmsman climbs on to the hull holding the leeward jib sheet and pulls the centreboard up into the fully lowered position. The crew can help by climbing on to the stern to break the suction. The helmsman, with back to the wind, leans back, pulling on jib sheet or centreboard. This should bring the boat into the semi-inverted position when you can proceed as before.

If this has not worked then try moving weight around the hull to break the seal. If the mast is stuck on the bottom you will need to get the safety boat to help you out.

Recovering a single-hander

With a capsize to leeward in a single-hander you can often avoid going into the water by climbing up the high side of the boat as it goes over and swinging a leg over on to the daggerboard. You can then right the boat again by leaning to windward and climb back in as it comes upright.

Man overboard recovery

This is a skill worth practising as not only would it be essential if the helmsman or crew were to fall overboard but it also brings together a lot of basic sailing skills and judgement. Practise it frequently and do not stop doing so once you start doing it well, particularly if you are sailing a different boat as handling characteristics vary tremendously. For practice find an area with plenty of unobstructed water and use something that floats low in the water that will drift as a person would. A bucket with a fender attached is popular but do not chuck out your only bailing bucket. Another option is a large and nearly full water container.

In Chapter 6 I described how a fine reach is the most controllable point of sailing for manoeuvring and this exercise is an important and typical example. Your aim, if you have lost someone over the side, is to get the boat under control as quickly as possible, keep sight of the person in the water and sail back to them on a fine reach with speed well under control so you can stop when you get there. It is no good charging back and running over the person in the water at 4 knots; better to take your time, stay calm and keep in control.

Man overboard step by step:

---

1 As soon as possible regain control of the dinghy, sheeting out everything and lying to for a few seconds if necessary to sort things out. Then head off on a beam reach. If your boat will manoeuvre well under mainsail alone then just leave the jib flying free, it is one less thing to worry about. Similarly have the centreboard about three-quarters down and leave that too.

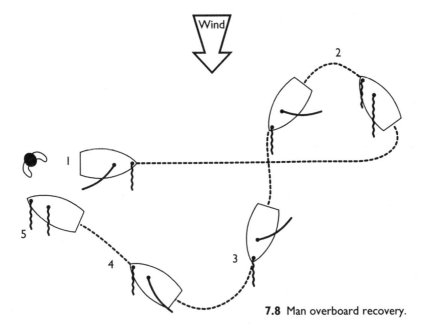

7.8 Man overboard recovery.

2 Tack when you have enough distance to give plenty of room on the way back to manoeuvre on to the right line. This comes with practice as you do not want to go so far that you lose contact with him. In a dinghy try about 50m (55yd) to start off with. Head back on a beam reach initially.

3 Bear away on to a broad reach in order to get downwind a bit. Remember you are aiming to be able to approach him on a fine reach. If you go too far downwind at this stage you will end up beating back to him. Not far enough downwind and you will still be on a beam reach and have trouble slowing down.

4 Approach on a fine reach, controlling your speed by spilling or filling your mainsail. If you have misjudged the angle of approach or are travelling too fast then sail past and return on the other tack for another attempt.

5 Stop the boat with the person in the water at the windward shroud. If you give the tiller a nudge up to windward at this stage you are less likely to end up tacking the boat round on top of them. You will now have stopped in the water with the sails flapping away and the boat lying to. Help the person aboard at the windward shroud (the above section on capsize explains why). If you have trouble with this use a loop of the windward jib sheet or a bowline tied in the end of it for him or her to step up on.

Anchoring

Some dinghy sailors never use an anchor and modern racing dinghies do not really have the space to carry one. This is quite sensible as they are heavy, only rarely used in sailing races and if you do retire it is unlikely it will be to stop for a picnic!

If you are sailing away from the watchful eyes of the safety boat then it is wise to carry an anchor, particularly if you are off for a day sail in coastal waters. It might be for planned use to temporarily secure the boat: a picnic perhaps or as a means of keeping the boat afloat when landing on a beach on a falling tide. It might also get used in an unplanned situation, after all you have not got any brakes on a dinghy so the anchor is considered essential safety equipment when cruising.

Types of anchor

There are many different types of anchor which have a variety of advantages and figure 7.9 shows those more commonly used on dinghies. Their holding power is in relation to the weight so the heavier you get the better for holding but do not load your boat up with more than you need.

The anchor should be stowed securely in the boat as you do not want it flying about on a bouncy day. Ideally it should have a short length of chain attached to it in addition to the anchor warp (rope). The chain's weight is important as it helps keep the pull on the anchor near horizontal. It also means the warp will suffer less abrasion on the sea bed. The warp should be of sufficient strength for the boat. A good permanent stowage arrangement is to have the warp on a drum but it could also be *flaked* into a bucket. When anchoring you need to know that the warp will run out without getting tangled so if it is not on a drum, flaking achieves this well. Tie the *bitter end* to a strongpoint in the boat (this can be the foot of the mast) then working from there fold the warp down into the bucket. When you get to the chain do the same until reaching the anchor which then stows in place.

Where to anchor

When choosing where to anchor there are several factors you need to consider, assuming you are anchoring in a sheltered location.

- What is the depth of water?
- What is the tide doing? How much will it rise or fall? (see Chapter 8)
- Which way will the boat lie (head to wind or tide) and where will it swing? Will it stay clear of other boats, moorings, main channel etc.?
- Avoid underwater obstructions such as mooring tackle, pipes and cables. (The latter are usually marked by yellow diamond signs ashore.)
- Going ashore? Unless you have got another means of getting ashore the simplest way is to sail on to the beach and anchor the boat by wading. On a falling tide wade out and drop anchor when you are waist depth. Do not forget to keep an eye on it if you do not want the boat to rest on the bottom. You can repeat the procedure as necessary if you are ashore for a long while. On a rising tide on a calm beach you can land ashore and carry the anchor up the beach a bit keeping an eye on it at intervals.
- Planning to leave the boat unattended? This needs very serious consideration, particularly with regard to changing weather and tide conditions. Are you supremely confident that the anchor will hold, the boat will not swing into anything and that you have fully considered what the tide is going to do? Will you be able to get

back on board later? You are unlikely to be able to answer all these questions until you have had some anchoring experience.

- Do you have enough warp for the depth you plan to anchor in? Try about five or six times the maximum depth of water when you are anchoring with a warp in reasonable conditions. Do not assume this is the right amount. The length of warp needed to hold the boat will vary with wind or tide strength, weight and type of anchor, the nature of the sea bed, etc. The message here is to check it is holding by sighting along a transit ashore. Conversely if it is calm, you are stopping briefly and keeping an eye on things then less warp might well do the trick.

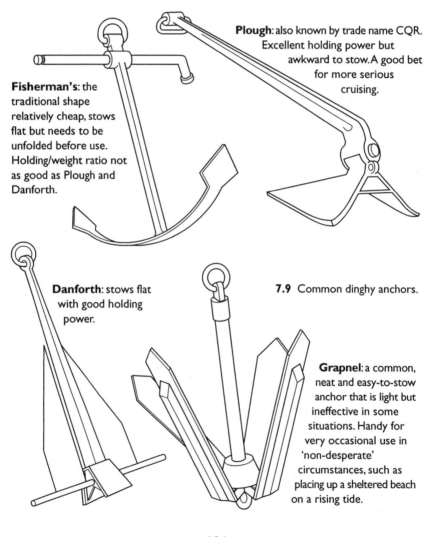

Plough: also known by trade name CQR. Excellent holding power but awkward to stow. A good bet for more serious cruising.

Fisherman's: the traditional shape relatively cheap, stows flat but needs to be unfolded before use. Holding/weight ratio not as good as Plough and Danforth.

Danforth: stows flat with good holding power.

7.9 Common dinghy anchors.

Grapnel: a common, neat and easy-to-stow anchor that is light but ineffective in some situations. Handy for very occasional use in 'non-desperate' circumstances, such as placing up a sheltered beach on a rising tide.

Anchoring techniques

Once you have decided where to anchor prepare the anchor with the warp running through a bow fairlead. These are found near the bow of some boats and are shaped guides for the warp to pass through. Large heavy dinghies may even have a bow roller which is a roller fitting right on the bow suitable for chain to run over. If your boat has neither of these then run the warp through a loop of line tied to the bottom of the forestay so it leads from the bow of the boat.

Anchoring is similar to picking up a mooring in that you are trying to bring the boat to a stop in relation to the ground. You do not have quite such a specific target but you have more considerations and decisions to make as to roughly where your target is. The methods of approach are similar to those for picking up a mooring (see pages 81–2).

Anchoring in slack water or with wind blowing in roughly the same direction as the tide:

- Approach on a close reach.
- Control speed by spilling wind.
- Come to rest at the chosen spot – go around again if you need to.
- Pay the anchor warp out smoothly as the boat starts to drift astern. Once the anchor is on the bottom a small amount of tension on it as it goes out ensures the warp is laid out correctly and helps stop the bow from being blown off to leeward.
- When you have paid out the required amount check the boat actually stops. Using a transit ashore (see Chapter 8) can help make sure of this.
- Lower the sails, raise the centreboard and tidy up.

Anchoring with wind against tide (expecting to lie head to tide):

- Sail upwind of the chosen place, luff up and lower the mainsail.
- Sail back downwind using just the jib, sheeting out to slow down as you come to the chosen place.
- Let the jib out completely to stop the boat and lower the anchor
- Pay out the required amount of warp as the boat drifts backwards on the tide.
- Find a transit ashore to check that the anchor is holding.
- Lower the jib and tidy up.

Sailing off the anchor

If wind and tide are similar to when you anchored use the same sail combination to sail off and reverse the process. Take in the warp slowly with the sail(s) hoisted and flapping. The crew should feel when the anchor comes off the bottom and the helmsman can keep a check on your transit which also tells you when you are no longer anchored. At that moment (or preferably just before) use the sails to sail off in the same way as when leaving a mooring (see pages 59–60).

If the anchor has caught on something on the sea bed and will not come up, then try and free it by pulling it from a different direction. If this does not work it may be that it is hooked around chain or a sunken object. The other method to try is to tie a loop of line around the warp and weight it with something. Let the line sink to the anchor while you are pulling the warp tight. Then slacken the anchor warp and pull on the line from different directions. This should lift the *flukes* of the anchor clear of the obstruction.

Occasionally when sailing out of a tight spot you might go out backwards. One way of doing this is by shortening the anchor warp until the anchor drags and the wind takes you astern. When you are ready you can sail off as described above. Alternatively you can sail backwards but it is best to practise somewhere uncrowded.

Sailing backwards

This is a technique only rarely used but is quite fun to practise and occasionally comes in handy. Start with the boat pointing into the wind, with the centreboard fully raised and the jib sheets free. If you have a daggerboard having it part lowered may help but the centreboard swivels aft as you raise it so it is probably better to raise it completely. Hold the tiller rather than the tiller extension and imagine sighting along it from the end you are holding looking out over the stern. To steer the right way face aft and point the rudder and the aft end of the tiller in the direction you want to go.

Push the boom out so that the mainsail is backed and the boat will start to sail backwards. Steering will become a little touchy and small tiller movements are called for. As the boat gathers speed the pressure on the rudder increases so a firm hand is necessary to prevent the rudder from slamming across potentially damaging the fittings. To get best control try different centreboard positions and adjusting boat trim to find what works best.

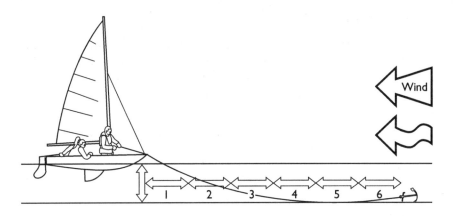

7.10 Length of warp.

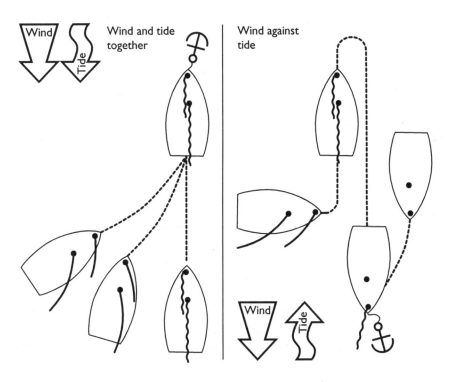

7.11 Anchoring techniques.

8

Basic coastal sailing

This chapter is not intended as a definitive guide to coastal sailing but does give essential information to those planning to start their sailing on tidal waters. Your sailing should start in a confined familiar area and away from strong tidal streams. One of the joys of coastal sailing however is the accessibility of larger expanses of water to explore. Most sailors are adventurous by nature and as the beginner progresses to a competent intermediate sailor then he or she will no doubt want to improve their skills and sail and explore further.

In this chapter, therefore, I hope also to provide an introduction for those wanting to go a little further, sail in stronger tidal streams, explore the estuary more or head away for a day sail on local waters in good conditions and in good visibility. The chapter does not cover skills for going more than half a mile from land or out along open coastlines for any distance and so does not cover the skills of navigation with compass and plotting instruments. Along with the joys of sailing at sea come a host of added dangers and describing how to undertake longer and more exposed coastal passages is outside the scope of this book.

Your sense of adventure should be tempered by an increasing awareness of what you yet need to learn and you will seek further training to match your skills with your ambitions. Advanced dinghy sailing courses such as the RYA level five course on the UK dinghy sailing scheme are particularly relevant to developing advanced practical skills and making appropriate coastal passages. For courses in other countires see the addresses on page 146.

Another way of building your knowledge of skills relevant to coastal sailing would be by attending a shore-based theory course in navigation. These are usually run in evening classes or as a one-week full-time course. They are theory courses only though and in the UK are part of the RYA Cruising Scheme. This means that they focus on information and techniques relevant to yachts equipped with chart table and navigational equipment not usually available to the small open boat sailor. They are also classroom based and the skills taught are not put into practice at sea.

If you are seriously interested in coastal cruising though, shore-based courses give an excellent amount of information. Such a course would help develop your seamanship and navigational understanding and at a beginner's level would require no prior knowledge to attend.

Planning

Any coastal trip will require good planning even if it is just a short trip locally. I have already covered the importance of using weather forecasts and the further you are from home the more important this becomes. You should plan for the weather forecasted but make sure you have thought out alternatives if the weather does not turn out as planned. Your idea of a beautiful day's sail in gentle winds and sunshine might turn into a nightmare if the wind increases by a point or two on the Beaufort scale. At the other extreme the wind might die altogether and leave you to row home as happened to me on my first dinghy cruise.

Simon and I were like big kids on their very own Arthur Ransome adventure. I had sailed yachts and larger boats to some wonderful places from the Channel Islands to the more remote islands of the Hebrides, but casting off in an open boat with a weekend's food and gear aboard opened up a whole new range of experiences. The weather was sunny as forecast as we reached away in a perfect force three wind. I hadn't sailed in Cornwall before but it proved to be an ideal first cruise for the boat and a beautiful and popular sailing area. It was not long before we were heading out past Pendennis Point doing serious damage to the chocolate biscuit supply. Our destination was the Helford River and this came quickly after we had identified and passed August Rock where we caught two mackerel. Tacking up to Helford Passage was great fun and we rowed up Port Navas Creek to find a quiet spot to rig the tarpaulin over the boom. Fortunately it did not rain that night as the tarpaulin arrangement was far from perfect but we had a great fresh mackerel supper and slept well. The morning dawned fine but with hardly a breath of wind. The log reads:

> *0945 Anchor aweigh, drifting out of Helford River, very light airs.*
> *1200 Still trying to drift out of Helford River. Better start rowing!*

We had a relaxing morning and had been hoping for something of a breeze to develop once we got out to more open water. I read and Simon fished but he had not caught anything. Midday was our cut off point and so we proceeded to row back, taking shifts on the oars. We finally cut our passage short six miles later at Flushing so Simon could hitch hike round to get the car and trailer.

It was a fair old row for a heavy boat and one of several that Simon became involved in on that boat. It became something of a joke that each trip might involve one of these lengthy stints at the oars but we saw it as part of the experience really. Occasionally the pressures of returning to work or catching a train got in the way and only then did I seriously come close to wishing I had an outboard motor. Obviously judging the weather becomes really important and being able to allow for being stormbound or coping with the prospect of a day long row depends on your freedom to adapt your plans accordingly. When Simon and I once faced a ten-hour row it was a potential nightmare and we only had ourselves to blame. We had been rather lazy and with a good wind forecast we had not got up in time to use all of a favourable tide. We were saved on that occasion by the wind returning in sufficient measure to push us back to our start point against the tide.

These examples are a bit beyond the day sails I envisage that you will be undertaking with this book but the main point is not to assume the conditions will remain constant and that you will be able to cover the same distance in the afternoon as you did in the morning. If wind is the only factor then it is often sensible to head upwind on the outward journey so you can return with the wind behind you. Bear in mind the wind forecast though and consider whether you expect the wind direction to change. You should also consider the tidal stream direction for the duration of your passage and depending on the relative strength of wind and tide it is often advisable to be able to head downtide on your return journey. This of course is much more predictable than the wind which can confound even the best laid plans.

Charts and pilotage

Part of your preparation for a day sail will be to make sure you have a good knowledge of the area you are planning to sail in. A large-scale chart of your area provides an ideal source of information about the areas of shallows, dangers, navigation marks and other features. Standard charts are expensive though and on a small boat the size of some can make them difficult to use. Small craft versions are also available which are folded into a more manageable size and contain navigational information printed on the reverse. If you are buying charts then see which types best cover the area you sail in.

For cruises away from familiar waters charts become essential but for the purposes of dinghy day sailing in familiar and straightforward waters

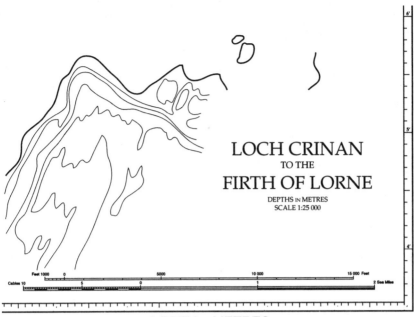

DEPTH IN METRES

8.1 Some chart projections allow the inclusion of a scale line.

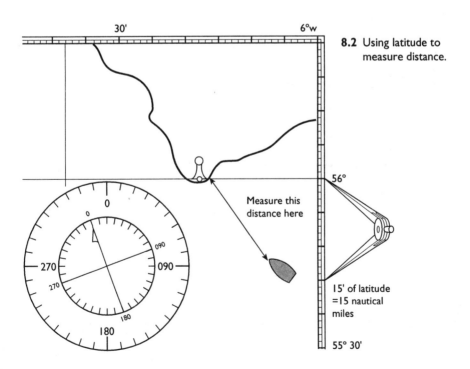

8.2 Using latitude to measure distance.

Measure this distance here

56°

15' of latitude = 15 nautical miles

55° 30'

it is possible to manage without a chart. The information they contain is nevertheless very important and looking at a chart of your intended sailing area should hold no surprises. Look carefully at the area you are going into and check for dangers such as rocks and shallows, building a picture of where they are. Charts are interesting to look at and so are often found on the walls of bars, marina offices, chandlery shops and sailing clubs. You may wish to make some notes in a form you will be able to understand and refer to. I find a notebook of waterproof paper quite handy for noting tides and other information I need. Some friends of mine, when going sea kayaking, pull out carefully notated maps with all the necessary information copied on. White acrylic boards can also be written on with waterproof felt pen or chinagraph pencil.

The first consideration on a chart is probably the scale and this varies from chart to chart. A large-scale chart shows a fairly small area in large detail, an example being a scale of 1:25 000. This means that 1cm on the chart represents 25 000cm (250m) of actual distance (or that 1in =

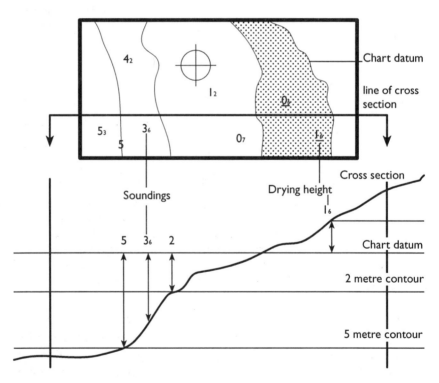

8.3 Chart soundings.

Rock which does not cover. Numbers refer to height above mean high water springs.

Rock with a drying height above chart datum.

Rock awash at the level of the chart datum.

Rocks or ledges covered by less than 2m of water at chart datum or those considered to be dangerous to surface navigation.

8.4 Some charted dangers.

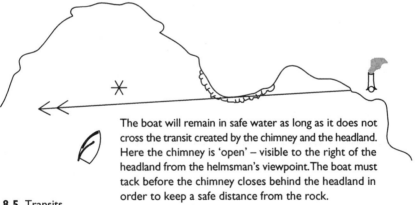

The boat will remain in safe water as long as it does not cross the transit created by the chimney and the headland. Here the chimney is 'open' – visible to the right of the headland from the helmsman's viewpoint. The boat must tack before the chimney closes behind the headland in order to keep a safe distance from the rock.

8.5 Transits.

25 000in, i.e. 694yd). Charts can come at even larger scales and 1:20 000 or 1:12 500 are also fairly common. Large-scale charts usually have a scale drawn on them showing the length of a nautical mile split into tenths that are called cables. Not all chart projections allow the use of a scale line, so distances on a chart are usually judged by reading the

latitude marks parallel to where you are measuring. One minute of latitude is equal to one nautical mile (see figure 8.2).

Once you have got an idea of the scale of the chart you are looking at then take a look at some of the detail. It provides a wealth of information and one of the most obvious is the depth of water. In tidal waters this changes, of course, and so the depths indicated relate to a specific level of tide that is called *chart datum*. This can be taken to be a low level, below which the tide rarely falls, so generally there is at least the depth of water indicated by the *soundings* which are given in metres and dotted around the chart. Certain lines of equal depth are joined together to produce depth contours. These vary according to the scale of the chart but typically might be at chart datum, 2, 5 and 10m. The shallower soundings are in tenths of a metre so 2_5 would be 2.5m. The edge of the land is the mean spring high water mark and the area between this and chart datum, like a beach which covers and uncovers with different tides, is called a drying area. Soundings here are measured above chart datum and called *drying heights*, denoted by an underline 1_3.

The chart is full of other information showing features both at sea and on the land which are useful to the sailor. Dangers are probably the most important and figure 8.4 shows the most common ways that rocks are indicated. Charts have a key to their symbols printed on the reverse, others – such as UK Admirality charts – have a separate booklet that provides the key.

The dangers in your area may well be marked by buoys so get to know the buoys and markers and make sure you know which side of the danger they are. In Europe the colours and shapes all conform to the IALA system which tells you where the safe water is in relation to the buoy. If you want to sail into new areas you will need to learn this system but for now you can just get familiar with the buoys in your area. Buoys mark the main channels for larger vessels so often are marking something that just is not a danger to a shoal draft boat like a dinghy. Check the detail on a chart and if in any doubt keep well clear.

On the other hand you may be sailing closer to unseen dangers that are not marked by a buoy or beacon and you will have to avoid them by using other means. The simplest is by remembering them in relation to features ashore such as a building or a particular section of coastline. You could remember that a rock lies 'about two cables offshore of the chimney' but this can be a little vague and it can be hard to judge distance across the water. It is much more accurate to use a couple of features on the shore to make a line that you avoid crossing. This is called a transit and can be printed on the chart or in pilot books or you can figure them out and draw them on for yourself (see figure 8.5). Transits provide the quickest and most accurate aids to the *pilotage* necessary to keep your boat in safe water. It is often necessary to combine more than one transit to use them to best effect.

Tides

The main difference between inland and coastal sailing is the tide and how it can affect just about everything you do. If you are heading for tidal water then you must be able to look up the tide and work out when you can launch, where you can go, how fast you might go and also where you should avoid.

Tides are caused by the gravitational pull of the moon and the sun and their effect on the earth in conjunction with the earth's rotation. When the moon, sun and earth are all in line they cause the larger spring tides; when the sun and moon are offset then smaller neap tides occur. It takes about 28 days for the moon to orbit the earth so there are about seven days between each of these phases.

Tide times can be looked up in almanacs, newspapers or in published

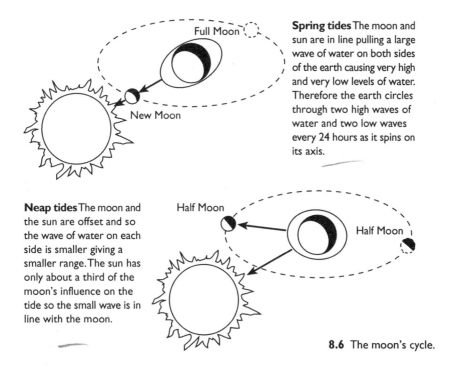

Spring tides The moon and sun are in line pulling a large wave of water on both sides of the earth causing very high and very low levels of water. Therefore the earth circles through two high waves of water and two low waves every 24 hours as it spins on its axis.

Neap tides The moon and the sun are offset and so the wave of water on each side is smaller giving a smaller range. The sun has only about a third of the moon's influence on the tide so the small wave is in line with the moon.

8.6 The moon's cycle.

booklets which are usually available in chandler's shops, bookshops and newsagents.

The format is normally as follows or similar:

```
0009    0.6
0609    4.3
1235    0.6
1826    4.1
```

Here the times are in 24-hour clock and the heights are in metres. You need to know whether the time given is local time or if you have to correct it for the relevant zone or for seasonal time changes. Often tide tables mark the days on which the moon is full or new, usually denoted by a circle for a full moon and a solid spot for a new moon. This is useful information as you will see that the spring tides follow these moon phases by about a couple of days. The above example shows a spring tide for Oban and has a morning range of 3.7m (12ft). A neap range can be as little as a metre (3ft) in Oban. It is worth examining the tables for your area to see what your average spring and neap ranges are.

Tidal information is specific to a place and will need to be adjusted if you are any distance away. The adjustments to be made to these standard port times and heights are usually also listed for a variety of other local places. It must also be remembered that these are predictions and that strong wind conditions and unusual weather patterns can affect them. For your purposes initially this approximate information is probably sufficient but take local advice from other sailors or fishermen as to the quirks of the tide in your area.

Bear in mind that tidal information can be considered as two separate but entirely related subjects. So far we have only really considered the height of tide or tidal rise and fall. This is likely to be most important when considering where and when to launch a boat. Some slipways cannot be used at all states of tide so you have to plan your launch and recovery accordingly. Another aspect of the rise and fall that may affect you is whether at low tide you have enough of an area to sail in! At Outward Bound Aberdovey in Wales the broad estuary at high water becomes rather a narrow ribbon at low water and this brings into consideration the second aspect of tides – *tidal stream*. This is the horizontal movement of water that can cause a real problem to a low-powered vessel such as an engineless sailing boat in light airs. As the tide falls at Aberdovey the sandbank is exposed and the ebbing tidal stream is concentrated in the remaining narrow channels. This increases the rate of the tidal stream to such an extent that sailing against it is often impossible. Such a place can be dangerous for an unsupervised beginner so if you are in tidal water take local advice, have someone ashore keep an eye on you and get your timing right.

When you are sailing on the coast it is important that you always know the state of tide – whether it is rising or falling and the times of high and low water. Knowledge of whether you are in a spring or neap tide period is also important as the greater the range the faster the tidal stream. Most (but not all) places have tides with a time difference of approximately six hours between high and low water. The tide does not fall evenly during that period though and it can be seen from figure 8.7 that during the third and fourth hours the tide falls a lot more than in the first and last hours. A general rule of thumb is the twelfths rule: In the first and last hour the tide drops one twelfth of the range = 0.5m. In each of the second and fifth hours the tide drops two twelfths of the range = 1m. In the middle two hours the fall is three twelfths per hour = 1.5m.

From this we can see that the greatest tidal change occurs mid-tide

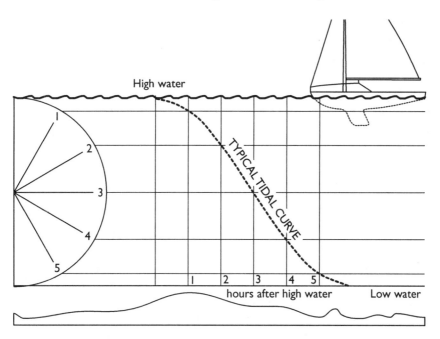

8.7 Tidal curve for a theoretical tide with a 6 metre range, a midday high water and 1800 low water. It would appear in the tide tables as: 1200 6.5, 1800 0.5.

and this tends to be reflected in the rate of tidal stream as well as the rise and fall. The mid-tide period therefore tends to have the strongest tidal stream. This 'rule' is very approximate and does not apply to all areas but as long as your local tidal curve has roughly the same shape then the twelfths rule can be used whenever you want an approximate idea of what the tide will be doing through its range.

Working with the tide

You should try to build up a picture of the tidal stream peculiarities in your area. Some things you can predict just by looking at the shape of the land around. Tidal streams, like river currents, will be strongest in mid channel or in the deepest water, and will be stronger around the outside of bends. Have a look for the tell-tail signs of tidal streams. Boats on swinging moorings will usually sit pointing uptide. Buoys have water 'piling up' on the uptide side and turbulence is formed downtide of fixed objects like jetties or mooring posts. Make use of this by staying in a strong tide in your favour or avoid it by seeking the shallower water or the edges of the channel when you are looking to sail against the tide.

Other tidal peculiarities are not so predictable and here it is best to resort to gaining some knowledge from those with experience who know the waters. You may be extending your use of your usual cruising area, going further or just using the stronger tidal streams to your advantage. In this case you probably have seen much of the area you plan to go into from the shore and may have built up a picture of how things change at different states of tide. It might be that you have travelled to a new area and it is then that information contained on charts and in pilot books becomes essential. Check whether there are any specific tide-related dangers that should be avoided. These might include tidal narrows where the tidal stream increases enormously, often creating back eddies and mini-whirlpools that can make for challenging sailing in good conditions. With the wind blowing against a strong tide these places become treacherous for a small boat with large standing waves and overfalls ready to put you in serious trouble. Sand bars can also vary from benign to treacherous according to the wind and tide conditions and these too warrant extra caution and good knowledge.

Even with local knowledge you can still judge things wrong as I discovered one day years ago when sailing out of Padstow on the north coast of Cornwall. The problem there is that the broad Camel Estuary becomes a narrow channel once the tide has fallen sufficiently to reveal the large sandbanks. Apart from reducing the sailing area this also causes strong tidal streams in the narrower channels. With a low tide in the middle of the day I could launch sometime before the harbour dried out and drift on the outgoing tide to sail out along the coast or in the mouth of the estuary. It was fairly simple then to get the flood tide back to Padstow at the end of the day. When high water was in the middle of the day however there was more potential for getting it wrong!

It was a great sail in sunshine and moderate winds. One of those days where everything seemed to be perfect – the boat responsive, the water warm, and the views terrific. I rigged and launched in record time and was ready to cast off less than an hour after leaving home just in time to see the sandbank cover as the tide rose. I was quite happy to be out for a slow relaxing sail and I was enjoying it thoroughly. The picnic was good, great to have a boat that can take a good hamper! I even caught some fish for my tea. At Rock on the other side of the estuary I saw a couple of friends lounging on the beach so I press-ganged them into coming off with me. Dallying on the way back made me late but I thought I should be in time to get back to Padstow before the tide would stop me.

Oh dear, how we can get it wrong sometimes! The wind which had been constant all day eased off so just sailing back from Rock was beginning to take too long. I could see the sandbank more visibly under the water and had to lift the centreplate to stay in the shallow water. All I was managing to do was to glide sideways hoping to find more wind but as I neared the Padstow shore I sailed to a standstill in the lee of the town. A couple of tacks just saw me going backwards so I headed across to the sandbank, dropped the jib and started rowing. With all the effort I could muster I could only just stem the tide which by now was very strong. I was wondering how long I would have to wait if I dropped anchor and dried out on the sandbank. This was going to take some time so I then considered leaving the boat on the beach, coming home and working out when it would float again on the evening flood tide. Then the obvious hit me. As a sailor of larger boats it had not struck me that in the sandbank lay the answer. With a little boat all I had to do was get out and pull it! Over on the sand I rigged a stern and a bow line so that I could pull Spylgarn behind and to the side of me in the deeper water and steer her a little against the tide. Wading in the soft sand was hard work but it felt good between my toes and my shorts proved to be the best gear to be wearing in the circumstances! I soon got uptide of the harbour entrance and it was then a simple matter to row, ferry gliding across the stream, down into the harbour and back to the slipway just in time to use the rough bottom end of it. I really earned my drink in the Harbour Inn that day.

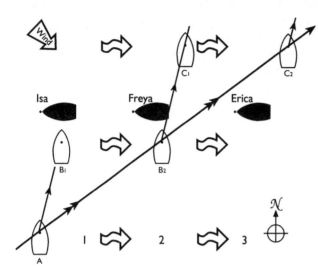

1. The boat is close hauled in a north-westerly wind and has a northerly heading. With leeway it may seem that she would move towards *Isa* at B1.

2. In fact the east setting tide takes the boat well clear to B2 where it looks as if she may clip the stern of *Freya*.

3. With good seamanship the helmsman has passed closely downtide of *Freya* with a ground track of B2–C2. Any misjudgement would result in being carried away from *Freya*. It is important here to keep well clear and uptide of any dangers or obstacles.

8.8 In this situation a boat is sailing across a tide setting strongly eastwards and the helmsman wishes to pass through a trot of moorings.

Manoeuvring in strong tidal streams

In referring to a strong tidal stream I mean one which has a significant effect on the course made good when sailing. Clearly this depends to some extent on the wind strength so there is no specific rate of tide to which this section applies. You will learn to judge the effect of the tide on your boat with experience. Start building that experience by choosing an area with moderate tidal stream well clear of any boats. The first thing to become aware of is the difference between the direction the boat is pointing in, the heading, and the direction you are travelling in. This has already come into your sailing to some extent when considering leeway and course made good. The tide will have an even more pronounced effect on the direction of travel and from here on I will refer to the *ground track* which describes the track taken over the sea bed (see figure 8.8).

The diagrams show clearly the progress made by a boat 'crabbing' sideways through the water but you are unlikely to have the same bird's eye view of the situation when you are at the helm. To help judge your progress and tell which direction your ground track is making you need to get used to finding transits to watch. We have seen how to use transits to aid pilotage and avoid dangers. Figure 8.9 shows how to use a transit to help steer through some moorings. The helmsman is using a

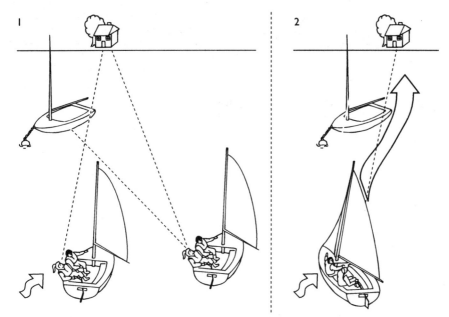

The boat is pointing (heading) towards the stern of *Freya* with a building in transit beyond. As the tide takes you from left to right the building appears to move to the right.

8.9 Steering on a transit.

Turn to port to compensate for the tide and watch the transit, steering a course to keep it in line. You now will follow the ground track you need but do not forget to alter course astern of *Freya* when you reach her.

building on the far bank, but it could be trees, shoreline features or boats on other moorings (but not boats under way!). To compensate for the tide, find a course that keeps your transit in line.

It is important that you know whether the wind is strong enough to achieve the planned course in the tide as otherwise you can get swept into all sorts of interesting predicaments! This is not for the beginner, but when you are happy with all the sailing manoeuvres sailing in tides can really sharpen your skills. When you have had some time sailing in stronger tidal streams away from boats and obstacles you will soon feel ready to manoeuvre amongst moored boats and then move on to sailing in more confined spaces. The main thing is to consider the possibilities of what might happen if things go wrong and allow for that in advance. When sailing amongst pontoons or jetties there is usually less space, more obstacles and with a tide running a whole new variety of ways that things can go wrong!

A approaches on a fine reach and takes the downtide berth keeping the boat sailing all the way in. Keeping the centreboard up reduces the ferry gliding to some extent but there is still a danger of landing further forward (upwind) than intended so allow plenty of room. In a strong tide with limited space in this situation there is nothing wrong with nosing slowly in to the pontoon bow first and securing a bow line before using lines to bring the boat alongside.

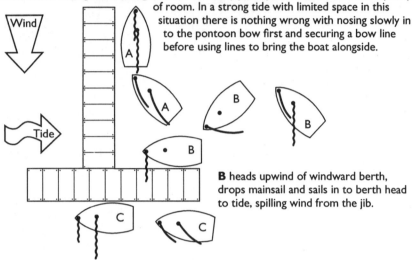

B heads upwind of windward berth, drops mainsail and sails in to berth head to tide, spilling wind from the jib.

C approaches head to tide onto a leeward berth, spilling wind from main and jib to slow down.

8.10 Approaching a pontoon – wind across tide.

Pontoons and jetties

You should always try to approach heading into the tide and consider how to keep the boom clear of the wall or jetty you are going alongside. This is generally done by not using the mainsail if spilling wind would swing it into the jetty. Alongside pontoons the boom is usually well above any obstructions, allowing a bit more flexibility, but if in doubt treat them the same as a jetty.

Coastal safety

Once you extend your sailing to the coast then some extra equipment is necessary to operate safely, particularly if you are sailing away from the cover of a safety boat. A checklist of equipment appears on pages 39-40 and is separated into the different relevant sections. The main thing to consider as a coastal sailor is to be independent and carry everything you need with you for the whole day. Have you got enough clothing to keep warm or hat, sunglasses and lotion to protect you from the sun? Cold, wind and sunshine all have a greater effect when you are at sea so you need to be suitably equipped for the prevailing conditions. The

A hoists both sails and lowers centreboard. The crew then pushes off the bow and the tide helps the boat sail clear of the pontoon by ferry gliding.

B needs to be aware that the tide will take the boat towards A berth but with both sails raised, centreboard down and a good shove off it should sail clear.

C has even less room and messes it up. As the boat drifts down towards the corner of A berth the helmsman tries to turn to starboard too far to avoid it. It stalls in the no-go zone and drifts sideways out of control. The helmsman should have moved forward to make more space, hoist sails and lower centreboard. Then with a manoeuvrable dinghy and a sharp crew, push off and keep the boat sailing with good speed through the water even if it is straight towards an obstacle. There would then have been enough boat speed to tack and sail clear, ferry gliding as A did.

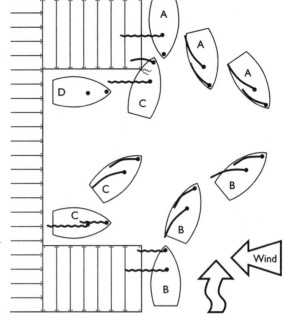

D looks pinned by the tide but in fact with both sails hoisted and centreplate down a good shove off allows the boat to sail clear, ferry gliding on the tide on a course made good that is parallel with A's.

8.11 Leaving a pontoon – onshore wind with cross tide.

coastal list includes a compass although I have not included use of a compass in the section on pilotage. This is because despite the fact that a compass is not necessary to work within the constraints of this chapter, I feel that it is worth having one on board if only to get used to how to use it for when you extend your trips. A steering compass is also useful when racing to help get the most from your boat. If you get things totally wrong and end up in poor visibility out of sight of landmarks then a compass can at least help you steer the boat in a straight line.

If you get into trouble that is life threatening then you need to know how to attract attention to summon help. There are a large number of internationally recognized distress signals you could learn but I shall describe only those relevant to the small boat sailor operating within the constraints of this chapter.

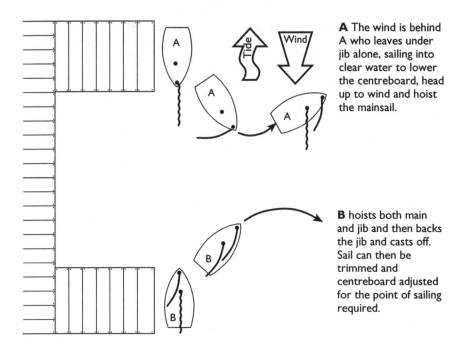

A The wind is behind A who leaves under jib alone, sailing into clear water to lower the centreboard, head up to wind and hoist the mainsail.

B hoists both main and jib and then backs the jib and casts off. Sail can then be trimmed and centreboard adjusted for the point of sailing required.

8.12 Leaving a pontoon – wind against tide.

Firstly if you do get into difficulty then stay with the boat. This is the most important thing to remember which you ignore at your peril. The boat will have a large amount of buoyancy to help support you in the water and furthermore presents a much bigger target if someone is looking for you. If you should become separated from the boat then just your head visible in the water will be difficult to spot. Distances at sea are difficult to judge and where you might feel quite happy swimming 1km (½ mile) in the swimming pool it is a different matter swimming in cold deep water, with the restrictions of clothes or wetsuit and buoyancy aid.

The standard distress signal that is applicable even on inland waters is to slowly raise and lower both arms outstretched. This is one that everyone on the water knows and will respond to. You can help draw attention to yourself by combining it with the audible signal of a whistle blast of SOS in Morse code (three short blasts followed by three long, then three short). Obviously this relies on being seen or heard so it is not wise to rely on in a coastal situation where your problem might be exactly that you are unable to return to the proximity of the shore, and other people and boats. For this reason I feel it is essential that any boat operating away from safety cover on coastal waters should carry flares. The basic minimum would be a couple of hand-held smoke flares, not buried deep in a locker but ideally in a waterproof container attached to the boat. The smoke flares I keep burn for 50 seconds and give off a large cloud of orange smoke. They are expiry dated and last for three years, but even after this there is a fair chance they will still work. For this reason, as well as two in-date smoke flares I keep a couple of recently expired ones as well. If you are in trouble then the more chance you have of attracting attention the better. These orange handsmokes are only of use in daylight and within a maximum of three miles from where you hope to be seen. Further offshore and in more remote situations parachute flares are necessary as they can be seen from a much greater distance. Therefore if you extend your cruising you will need to extend your flare supply as well.

Should you see another boat in distress then you have a responsibility to make sure that help is despatched as quickly as possible.

You should only consider going yourself to a boat in trouble if it is within the usual limits of your area sailing and if you do not put yourselves at risk by doing so. You also have to consider whether as a small engineless sailing boat you will be more effective by raising the alarm than by going to them when you will have limited space aboard to take people off and little power to tow. If you are the only people who have spotted the casualty and you sail off to help only then to discover you

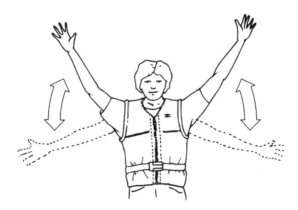

8.13 Raising and lowering arms is a recognized way of indicating distress.

cannot do so, then you will have delayed effective rescue by quite some time. Also bear in mind your own skill level and whether you may cause more problems than you can solve. As a general guide I would suggest that as an inshore dinghy sailor you only go to a boat in trouble if you are close enough to tell the size of it, its position and likely problem and can make a judgement as to whether you can help or not.

If the boat is some distance away and perhaps all you see is a smoke flare then your priority must be to call the coastguard. Remember the approximate position of the vessel and get ashore to the nearest house or phone to call the coastguard. If you are sailing in the vicinity of larger boats such as a yacht or motor cruiser, fishing boat or work boat then sail across to raise their attention. They probably have a VHF radio and will be able to call the coastguard direct and possibly provide assistance themselves.

The primary role of the coastguard is to coordinate marine search and rescue and they would take over the responsibility of directing the help available. They decide whether to call a helicopter or lifeboat or to use the other vessels in the area. If the phone is your method of contacting them then do not hesitate to call. They would rather have ten reported sightings than none at all because everyone thinks someone else will call. They might even build up a better idea of the location of the casualty if they have several sightings to go on. The other main distress signals you may come across are red, hand-held, burning flares and red parachute flares used for inshore distress at night and distress offshore respectively.

It should be remembered that the aim of this chapter is to provide a little extra knowledge for those people developing their sailing skills by coastal sailing. It has merely scratched the surface of the subject but it should have whetted your appetite for more knowledge and helped you become aware of the need to operate safely and go on learning.

9

Safety matters

Safety must be the prime consideration of all people involved in outdoor activities and so is the most important topic in the book. On an Outward Bound course each activity has its own safety brief and tutors put a clear emphasis on this. Whilst expecting the group to pay close attention to safety and look after each other, the tutor will also keep an eye on them with a view to safety at all times.

This provides a good 'safety net' and you can expect the same attention at any nationally accredited sailing school. Do not forget, however, that the whole point of this book is to get you off sailing without the instructor and eventually perhaps away from the watchful club rescue boat. This chapter covers general safety and in the rest of the book you will find many safety points and tips so you, like the watchful instructor, can try to pre-empt problems before they occur.

As you are not going to be watched over though you will have to take responsibility for your own safety. I believe that in the 'cotton wool wrapped' world we live in today this responsibility is taken away from the individual more and more and you may have to re-learn an approach that keeps you out of trouble. Good instructors learn to look out for critical safety for extended periods as a matter of course. This is done by being a safety pessimist at all times. Be positive and aim for the best but always consider the worst that might happen and either amend the plan or make a conscious decision to proceed having noted the danger.

Whilst I want to focus your mind on safety I do not wish to alarm and it must be stressed that sailing is a very safe sport when conducted properly. As you learn more you will decide which side of the sport is for you and you will become comfortable in operating in the new environment. The racing sailor needs to be happy that his or her equipment is in good order and can stand up to the stresses a hard racing season imposes. A racer needs to be confident operating at high speed in close proximity to other craft that might be fast and powerful and will be intent on getting the upper hand. The cruising sailor will wish to be more independent in order to safely sail away from the cover of the club rescue boat. Chapter 8 dealt with many safety points for the cruising sailor, particularly in coastal situations. The sailor who cruises on large stretches of inland water will also find useful information there. Many people enjoy both racing and cruising and find both activities rewarding. They will make a boat go faster and more efficiently when racing and extend the boundaries of their adventures when cruising.

Safety considerations:

- Make sure personal kit is in good repair and that you foresee eventualities or a change of plan. Have with you everything that you need. Use the checklists (see pages 39-40) or adapt them.
- Are the boat and equipment in good repair? Gear failure can be serious so good maintainance is essential. Develop a maintenance checklist and keep everything in good working order.
- Is your planned activity well considered and thought through? Have you got all the information? Have you considered the potential ways and occasions things could go wrong? To do this think through the immediate factors of you, your boat, your crew and your equipment, and the external factors of weather, tides, hazards, and other vessels etc.

As well as immediate and external factors there will be both anticipated events and unpredictable events. The relation between these can be shown by the examples in the following table.

Possible problems to consider

Anticipated events

Immediate factors
Hunger, thirst, coldness, tiredness, avoiding injury by careful, skillful operation, avoiding gear failure by good maintenance.

External factors
Tidal constraints and dangers, onset of darkness, lee shores and shoreline hazards, weather – e.g. forecast wind change. Avoiding vessels in busy shipping areas.

> **Unpredictable events**
>
> **Immediate factors**
> Coping with injury/illness coping with gear failure, capsize.
>
> **External factors**
> Weather not as forecast.
> Danger from other vessels.

These are some examples of potential problems to consider and you may well think of more that are relevant to your specific situation. Not everything in life can be categorized and some things here fall into more than one area. Weather conditions for example can be anticipated through forecasts and understanding of local effects but might turn out to be rather different. You therefore have to plan bearing in mind both the forecast and how things would be for you if the weather turns out differently. Perhaps we should call this an area of 'anticipatable unpredictability'!

Considering the potential problems is useful but we should also look at how to avoid them or be prepared to cope with them if they occur.

How to avoid or minimize anticipated problems:

- Thorough preparation – being properly equipped with boat and gear in well maintained condition.
- Good planning which keeps you aware of the external factors and helps you to operate within safe margins.
- Good judgement and careful operation – ensuring that things remain in your control and within the bounds you had planned.

Unpredictable problems are obviously harder to avoid. The likelihood of injury or gear failure as two examples can be lessened but not ruled out.

How to reduce the risk of unpredictable problems:

- Reduce the possibilities of such problems occurring by careful operation and good maintenance.
- Lessen the impact of problems should they occur by awareness (noticing problems at an early stage) and training (capsize recovery, first aid, etc.).

Consider the potential outcome of problems to give some way of judging the seriousness of the activity. For example a capsize during a club race has little risk with a safety boat ready to give assistance if necessary. A capsize when cruising away from a patrolled area could have a much greater risk.

Training and awareness – some specific situations

Many situations can be prepared for by some of the learning discussed in this book. If you have practised sailing without a rudder for example it will not be such a disaster if it ever breaks, and you should be well practised in capsize and man overboard recovery. Some other potential problems need expanding on.

The lee shore

This inspired dread in sailors of old when ships might founder by failing to make to windward. We must still look on this with similar caution despite the efficiency with which most modern boats now sail close hauled. If the wind should rise beyond the level you can sail with smallest mainsail, if the waves stop you from making to windward, or if something goes wrong and you lose drive, then you would quickly drift downwind. If that takes you towards a rocky shore with breakers you are in big trouble. Even a gentle sloping shoreline in moderate wind should be regarded with caution so always think through the considerations of a lee shore when sailing.

Being towed

If you need a tow, unless it is a simple situation with the club rescue boat then it is usually better to use your own painter or towline. Usually people are keen to help but if an unknown boat gives you a tow then salvage laws could give them a claim so you should bear this in mind. The failsafe is to negotiate a fee before passing the towline.

A towline should be made fast to a strongpoint on the boat, often the foot of the mast is a good place. You should be able to undo the line when it is loaded. A round turn and two half hitches would be suitable (see page 30). Ideally the painter should go through a fairlead on the bow. The sails should be lowered, the centreboard raised at least half way and you should steer to follow the boat towing, sitting towards the stern.

Other vessels

This comes into a fairly predictable category as a straightforward hazard where danger is avoided by a defined set of rules. These are the

International Regulations for the Prevention of Collision at Sea (collision regs for short). The result of a collision with another vessel could vary from a minor embarrassment to a tragic loss of lives and boats. Every boat user should therefore have a working knowledge of the priorities between vessels and how to avoid collisions.

International Regulations for the Prevention of Collision at Sea (IRPCS)

The first priority in any close quarters situation is to assess whether a risk of collision actually exists. In the case of two dinghies this is fairly easy and once you are experienced you can allow them to come fairly close to one another. When racing, sailing boats come particularly close together and use International Yacht Racing Rules to avoid contact as well. For the moment though a basic knowledge of the collision regs will suffice. If you are judging risk of collision with a larger vessel some way off then hold a steady course and line up the vessel with a part of your boat. If the ship continues to be in line with that shroud or rowlock or whatever you have used then there is a risk of collision.

Collision avoidance basics:

- You are required to keep clear of a ship manoeuvring in a narrow channel. This might be a stretch of water that seems quite broad to you but may be fairly tight for a ship with deep draught. You should keep clear of larger vessels anyway and do not expect ships to give way to you in restricted waters.

- If you are proceeding along a narrow channel then you should keep to the starboard side. If you wish to cross a channel you should do so by heading straight across at right angles.

- An overtaking vessel is required to give way to one being overtaken. This includes you if you are sailing past a motor boat slower than you.

In the case of any other situation where risk of collision exists a list of priorities determines who gives way to whom.

Who has right of way?

- The simplest of these is that power gives way to sail (do not forget the above rules though). Be aware that some water users are not very good at responding to this or even might not know the rules at all!
- Between two sailing vessels the right of way is with the boat on the starboard tack.
- If sailing vessels are on the same tack then the boat to windward gives way. This is best done by passing astern of the boat to leeward.

The boat with right of way must hold a steady course to enable the give way vessel to avoid it. If the give way boat does not take action in time then the boat with right of way should take avoiding action. There is no point in being obstinately in the right if you end up getting run down!

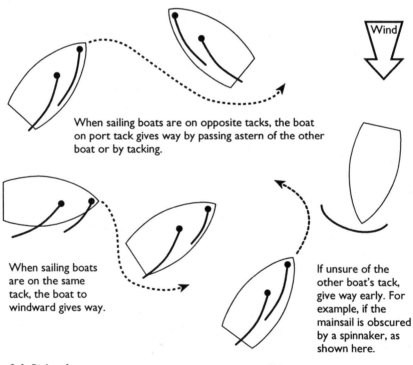

Wind

When sailing boats are on opposite tacks, the boat on port tack gives way by passing astern of the other boat or by tacking.

When sailing boats are on the same tack, the boat to windward gives way.

If unsure of the other boat's tack, give way early. For example, if the mainsail is obscured by a spinnaker, as shown here.

9.1 Right of way.

First Aid

No responsible person should head for the great outdoors until they have been on a recognized first aid training course, and nobody involved in outdoor activities should lead others without a thorough working knowledge of first aid techniques. Many sailing courses contain an element of first aid procedures, but this is often very basic. The Red Cross, the St John Ambulance and the St Andrew's Ambulance Association all run excellent courses and the telephone number of your nearest local branch can be found in the telephone directory. Many of the key techniques used in first aid – especially mouth-to-mouth ventilation and chest compression – cannot be learned from books and must be practised under the supervision of a qualified trainer. Books, including this one and the more detailed *Outward Bound First Aid Handbook*, should be regarded as reference works rather than as substitutes for training.

Often the best emergency first aid action is to do nothing at all, other than minimize the danger to the patient and other members of the crew, and seek qualified help at once. You can do a great deal of harm by over-enthusiastic medical treatment. On a boat, this principle is even more important than on land because you may be faced with rapidly changing circumstances in which external factors demand your attention and potentially pose a threat to everyone on the boat. In stormy weather, for example, the demand of managing the boat to ensure the safety of all crew members may be more important than attending to the casualty. If you neglect your seamanship and go aground or capsize then you will not have done anyone any favours. In fact you may have removed the quickest means of transporting the casualty towards professional medical assistance.

Establishing priorities

Consequently, the emphasis in your first aid should be to:

- Protect yourself and other crew members.
- Make the boat safe.
- Protect the casualty from further danger.
- Send promptly for qualified help.
- Promote the recovery of the casualty, if this is within your knowledge and means.

Safety

Your first thought when approaching any victim is to make the accident area safe for yourself and other people. For example: if the casualty was hit on the head by the boom, it will help nobody if you allow the same thing to happen to you. Take action to make the boat safe before attending to the patient. Check all around and above the victim for any signs of danger. Switch off the electrical current, activate fire alarms or open windows to release any smoke or fumes. Only once all risks have been eliminated, approach the casualty.

Never move a patient with a spinal injury, except as a last resort. If it is essential that the victim be moved at once (because their head is in the water, for example) great care must be taken, especially if it looks as though the victim has a damaged neck or spine. Quick indicators of a possible spinal injury are the nature of the accident, the position in which the victim is lying, and the lack of any sensation in the limbs.

When turning or lifting a victim with a suspected spinal injury:

- Use at least three or four people acting together.
- Move head, trunk and legs together, keeping the head supported.
- Avoid any rotation or bending of the spine.

A victim who needs to be moved can be rolled (as shown in figure 9.2) onto a stretcher or board (if available). Moving a spinal victim is best left to experts, and unless there is a very immediate risk to life and limb, it is better not to attempt this at all.

Assessing the casualty

The next step is to perform a body check to ascertain the actual damage. To a large extent this is the most important element of first aid. It may be necessary to remove the victim's lifejacket in order to perform resuscitation, but never leave a patient alone without their jacket.

The very first question you need to ask is whether the patient is conscious or not. If more than one patient is injured, always attend to the unconscious ones first; your priority being to see that they can breathe.

9.2 The correct way to turn or lift a victim with a spinal injury.

Remember your priorities by the maxim
Airway, Breathing, Circulation (ABC):

- Airway
  If the casualty is unconscious check that the airway is clear. Noisy breathing is an indication that the airway is blocked. Remove from the mouth any obstruction, such as loose dentures or mud. Tilt the head back by gently lifting the chin; this will clear the tongue from the back of the throat and open the airway.
- Breathing
  Place your ear near the victim's mouth. Can you hear breathing or feel any breath on your cheek? While doing this place your hand gently on the abdomen and look along the body. Can you feel the abdomen rising and falling or see the chest doing the same?
- Circulation
  At the same time feel for the victim's pulse by placing your fingertips (not thumb) on the neck, just behind the Adam's apple, in the gap between the windpipe and the muscle alongside it.

If the three ABC checks show a problem with the breathing or circulation then you need to take immediate action. If you cannot detect a pulse, waste no time in seeking help. Head for shore and get to the nearest telephone to call an ambulance, leaving the patient alone if necessary (this is the *only* occasion on which you should consider leaving the patient alone). On returning to the patient, give mouth-to-mouth ventilation and chest compression until help arrives (these lifesaving techniques are designed to maintain the oxygen supply to the brain until the medical team arrives). To learn how to use these resuscitation techniques, you should attend a first aid course.

Near Drowning

With sailing casualties, there is the very real risk of liquid getting into the victim's lungs and preventing them from breathing properly. The most common cause of near drowning is when muscle coordination is lost in cold water immersion. In this situation the casualty can no longer swim and sinks, inhaling water. Drowning can also happen almost instantly when the body gasps involuntarily when entering cold water. In this situation water is drawn into the lungs and the casualty loses consciousness within a few seconds. Usually only a small amount of water actually enters the lungs – unconsciousness results from a throat spasm that prevents the patient from breathing properly. Water inhalation is clearly not a healthy situation but is not always fatal. There have been cases where a casualty has been resuscitated with advanced life support systems after a period of up to an hour of being submersed in cold water. This happened with little or no resulting brain damage because of the onset of hypothermia, which offers temporary protection to the brain suffering oxygen deprivation.

A casualty who has been recovered from the water but is not breathing should be given mouth-to-mouth ventilation, also known as expired air resuscitation (EAR). There is no need to drain water out of the lungs as the water does not readily drain out. That which you do see coming out of the mouth has come from the stomach rather than the lungs. If there is no pulse then cardio-pulmonary resuscitation (CPR) should be given but be careful when assessing pulse if hypothermia has been a factor. In this case, the pulse is very weak and difficult to find but it is important to be sure no pulse is present even if it takes a couple of minutes, rather than risk damaging a functioning heart that has been slowed by hypothermia. Having been given EAR or CPR, all near-drowning patients should be treated as suffering from hypothermia: wet clothing should be replaced and the patient should be insulated from the cold (see pages 142–3).

Again, the benefits of attending a first aid course and learning the techniques of EAR and CPR cannot be overstressed. Most people who survive drowning have a working heart and respond to EAR within the first two minutes. Those needing CPR have a much lower survival rate. In either case, the casualty must go to hospital even if they do appear to have made a good recovery. The water acts as an irritant in the lungs and can cause serious respiratory problems later.

The body check

If the victim is fully conscious, and there are no problems with the ABC checks, continue with the body check. This is simply a case of working down the body and looking for signs of injuries. While doing so you should talk to the casualty (do this even if they are unconscious; they may be much more aware than you think). Reassure them, explain what you are doing and ask them to tell you if anything you do hurts them. Watch their face to see if the expression changes as you touch different parts of the body. Ask for the history of the accident if you did not witness it yourself, and ask whether anyone else was involved. Always remember that the obvious injury may not be the life-threatening one.

Head

Always start at the head. Look for any obvious injury and check for blood or fluid coming from the ears or nose which might indicate damage inside the skull. Check the eyes for foreign bodies or damage and the pupils for comparative size and reaction to light (which might indicate concussion). Feel if the skin is hot, cold, clammy or dry. These, together with other signs, could suggest hypothermia, heatstroke and/or shock. Finally be aware of the breathing: is it fast or slow, deep or shallow, and is it regular or struggling?

Neck

Move down to the neck and feel around for any obvious injury or dampness from bleeding. Check to see if the casualty is wearing a warning medallion such as those worn by diabetics or epileptics. Be aware of the pulse rate.

Trunk

Working on both sides of the trunk, press the ribs in carefully to see if there is a reaction by the victim which would indicate a chest or rib injury. Feel for abnormal hardness in the abdomen. Feel under the back for obvious injury, deformity or dampness from bleeding.

Limbs
Work along the arms and then the legs feeling for any unusual limb position, swelling, or bleeding. Check for a warning bracelet indicating diabetes, epilepsy, etc. See if the casualty can move their arms, legs, fingers and toes. If not, ask where the pain or difficulty lies.

Diagnosis
This body check only takes a few minutes, but it could be a lifesaver. Having made the check you are in a better position to inform the rescue services of the likely nature of the problem, so that they can gauge the level of their response.

The recovery position
Once the initial checks have been completed, the victim needs to be placed in the recovery position - unless suffering from a spinal injury (see page 134) - to prevent them choking on their own vomit or ingesting the acids produced by the stomach.

Kneeling beside the casualty, straighten the legs. Place the arm nearest to you at right angles to the casualty's body, then bend the upper arm parallel to the body, with the palm facing up. All the time ensure that the head is kept tilted back and the airway clear. Bring the arm furthest away from you across the casualty's chest and place their hand against the cheek nearest to you, with the palm facing outwards. This will cushion the patient's face and head when they are rolled over. Using your other hand, hold the thigh furthest from you and, keeping the casualty's foot flat on the floor, draw up the knee. Keeping the casualty's hand pressed against their cheek, pull the raised thigh towards you. This will roll the casualty neatly into the correct recovery position.

Ensure that the head is kept tilted back and supported on the casualty's hand. Once in this position the casualty should be wedged to prevent them from rolling with the boat. They should never be left alone but should be closely monitored for breathing problems, pulse rate, skin colour and condition, and the state of their consciousness – all of which could indicate a change in their condition.

Getting help
Prompt action on the part of trained medics is the key to preventing the loss of life in emergencies. Well-equipped cruising dinghies or yachts

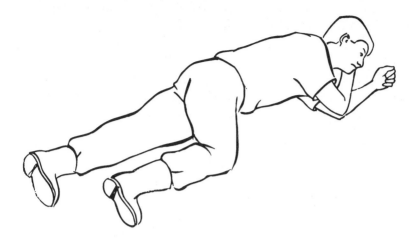

9.3 The recovery position.

carry a VHF radio and are able to summon assistance immediately either through the coastguard or other vessels. As a progressing sailor you should consider investing in a VHF set to add to your safety equipment for coastal cruising. Although not encouraged by the coastguard, mobile phones can also be useful to call for help. Be sure that the batteries are fully charged and that the telephone is protected from wet and damage by wrapping it in padding and plastic bags. Be sure that members of your party know where the telephone is, how to use it, and what numbers to call to summon help.

If you are unable to take these precautions, you need to head for shore as quickly as possible. On landing, you should ideally choose two competent members of your party to summon help, while the remainder stay with the casualty. Of course, if there are only two of you, the decision whether to stay with or leave the patient is extremely difficult, and will depend on factors such as the weather, how far you are from habitation and the nature of the patient's injuries. If you stay with the patient, you can use a whistle or torch to attract attention. (Six long blasts or flashes are the internationally recognized distress calls; these are answered with three short blasts or flashes).

Make sure that those who go to summon help know the patient's precise location. If you are unsure of your exact position, you can at least make a note of prominent landmarks in the area and take compass bearings from them find your approximate position.

**Be prepared to give the following information
to the rescue services:**

- Numbers and names of casualties.
- Precise location.
- Your assessment of the nature of their injuries.
- The age, condition and state of mind of the casualties.
- The time of the accident and the weather conditions at the scene.

Specific procedures

Once you have sent for help you can begin to treat the patient's injuries.

Bleeding

Blood loss should be attended to rapidly. Internal bleeding is revealed by a number of signs, which may include bruising, discolouring and/or bleeding from the body openings. There is little you can do to treat internal bleeding except for treating the shock that will almost certainly accompany it (see pages 141-2).

The treating of external bleeding is more straightforward. Remember two things: elevation and direct pressure. Elevating the wound will help to slow the rate of blood flow. Direct pressure can be applied to the wound with anything available. In the case of major bleeding, hygiene comes a low second so do not be afraid to use your hand tight against the wound or use a dirty rag, if that is all that is available; any risk of infection can be worried about later.

Get a dressing on the wound straightaway, but do not bind the wound too tightly; your aim is to stop the bleeding, not cut off the blood supply to the limbs. If blood starts to seep through the first dressing, place another dressing directly on top of it. Do not remove the first dressing.

Burns

There is only one first aid treatment for burns, no matter what the severity: the whole wound should be immersed in cold, preferably running, water. Remove anything that is in the way of the burn (clothing, rings, watches and so on) but never try to remove anything that is actually sticking to the burn, such as clothing. The wound area should be left in the water for at least 10 minutes, and considerably longer for anything more than a very minor burn. Do not stop treatment just because the wound stops hurting; keep it in the water for a good few minutes after that. Prompt treatment of even a serious burn will have dramatically beneficial effects.

Never apply lotions, ointments or creams to any burn. One of the worst misapprehensions in first aid is that fat (such as butter or margarine) cools a burn. This may be the initial effect but the longer term effect is that the wound literally cooks in the fat.

If the skin on the burn is not broken, it should be left open to the air. If the skin is blistered or broken, use a clean, light dressing made of non-fluffy material to cover the wound and keep out infection. Plastic kitchen film makes an ideal burns dressing, or you could use a clean plastic bag.

Scalds, caused by hot liquids, should be treated in the same way. Treat any burn victims for shock (see below) and keep a close check that the airway does not become obstructed while the patient is lying down to recover.

Sunburn

Prevention is far better than cure for this condition, so wear protective clothing and use sun blocks on exposed and vulnerable areas, such as the back of the neck, the face and lips, and the feet. After-sun lotions and calamine lotion will help to relieve minor burning.

Shock and hypothermia

These conditions can be killers in their own right. They can also be the underlying (and more serious) problem in an accident.

Shock

With anything more than a minor injury or accident, it is safe to assume that the patient will have suffered some degree of shock. As well as the actual casualty, other members of the crew should be closely monitored in case they, too, develop the symptoms of shock.

The initial signs of shock are:

- A rapid pulse.
- Pale, grey skin. A fingernail or earlobe, if pressed, does not regain its colour immediately.
- Sweating and cold, clammy skin.

As the shock develops, patients will become weak, giddy and nauseous. They may vomit, and their breathing becomes rapid and shallow. The pulse continues to be fast but irregular.

If the patient is not treated, they will become restless, anxious or aggressive. They may suffer 'air hunger', yawning and gasping for air. In the most severe case they may become unconscious and eventually the heart will stop beating.

The treatment for shock is surprisingly simple and effective. First, treat the obvious cause of shock, such as bleeding or burns. Lie the casualty down, keeping the head low and raising the feet to aid the supply of blood to the brain. Loosen any tight clothing, belts or equipment. Keep the casualty warm and insulated, give them plenty of reassurance and send for help.

Do not let the casualty move about, eat, drink or smoke. If they complain of being thirsty, moisten their lips with water.

Hypothermia

Hypothermia or exposure, as it is commonly known, is one of the great killers among those who pursue outdoor activities, but it can usually be avoided. It is caused by a combination of wet and cold, which can be aggravated by factors such as tiredness, inadequate clothing, inadequate diet and physical and mental attitude. Prevention is largely a matter of common sense.

Before sailing ensure that:

- All members of the group are correctly clothed and equipped.
- Everyone has eaten well, and that there is an adequate supply of food and drink (including emergency rations) on board.
- The weather conditions are suitable for your planned trip.
- The planned trip is within the physical and mental capabilities for all members of the group.
- Nobody in the group is suffering from a severe cold or flu or any other condition which makes the planned trip unsuitable for them.

While sailing, and at all times on the trip, crew members should keep an eye on each other. No matter how bad the conditions get, it is vital to try to keep talking to each other. Hypothermia often goes unnoticed until too late because crew members become enveloped in their own private world.

The signs of hypothermia include:

- Shivering and cold, pale marble-like skin.
- Apathy, confusion and irrational or 'drunken' behaviour.
- Complaining of tiredness, coldness, cramp (particularly in the calf muscles) or blurred vision.

Many of these symptoms could also be attributed to being merely 'cold, wet and tired'. The key to early recognition of hypothermia depends upon knowing the members of your crew and detecting behaviour that is out of character. The later signs, such as loss of faculties and blurred vision, are more obvious but the patient's health will already have deteriorated by the time these symptoms are displayed, and the aim is to arrest hypothermia at a much earlier stage.

The treatment for hypothermia:

- Provide shelter from the elements. The priority is to get the casualty out of the wind or rain.
- Provide insulation from above and below.
- Start gentle rewarming. Placing another person in a sleeping bag with the casualty is a good method.
- Send for help.

You should never give the patient alcohol; nor should you attempt to rewarm the casualty rapidly by rubbing the skin or applying hot water bottles or any other form of direct heat. Give the patient a hot drink, soup or small amounts of high-energy food, such as chocolate, so long as there are not abdominal injuries. If there are other injuries, be cautious about food and drink but remember that hypothermia is often a bigger problem than the injury that started the situation. Wet clothes should only be removed in a warm sheltered environment and only if there are dry clothes immediately at hand.

Always assume that you and the other members of the group are also suffering from the initial stages of hypothermia and treat everyone accordingly. Remember: shelter, warmth and high morale are what you need to maintain while you wait for help.

Heat exhaustion

Heat exhaustion results from dehydration and salt loss because of excessive sweating. It can be caused by other conditions, such as diarrhoea or vomiting. Patients suffering from heat exhaustion will complain of dizziness, headaches, cramps and loss of appetite or nausea. The skin will be clammy, sweaty and pale. Move the patient to cool, shaded surroundings, preferably with a breeze. Help the patient to lie down, then raise and support the legs to promote blood flow to the brain. Give the patient as much salt solution (2 teaspoons of salt per 1 litre/2 pints of cool water) as they can drink. If recovery is slow, or if the patient's breathing and pulse remain rapid, seek immediate medical advice.

Fractures

In the case of a minor fracture (for example, of the arm, fingers or collar bone), the fracture should be supported in whatever position the casualty finds most comfortable and restrained from further movement. Fingers can be strapped to each other, while a broken arm can be supported in a sling and then strapped to the body. A collar bone is treated in the same manner as if the arm on that side were broken. Minor foot, leg or ankle injuries can be treated similarly.

If the fracture cannot be treated in this way, make the patient as comfortable as possible and summon help. If it is necessary to immobilize a limb to prevent the condition becoming worse, the best option is to use other body parts – strapping the legs together, for example. To do this, place cushioning material between the legs, especially at the knees and ankles, then bandage the legs together, tying the knots on the side of the uninjured leg. Check the bandages are not too tight by pinching a toe nail: if it stays pale, loosen and retie the bandages.

Do not give food or drink to the patient, in case they need an emergency operation to reset the bones.

Dislocations

Dislocations can be very painful and require expert help. Some people have a history of dislocations and sometimes know how to treat themselves by pushing the joint back in. This is very rare and is not something you should attempt.

Chronic conditions

You should always be aware if any member of your party suffers from a chronic condition such as asthma, diabetes or epilepsy. In each case it is vital that you know how to deal with any problems that might arise, and that you have adequate supplies of medicines and inhalers. Asthma sufferers should carry and use their own inhalers rather than a communal one.

Bites and stings

Bites and stings vary greatly from the intense annoyance caused by the Scottish midge to the lethal effects of some snakes and marine life.

Black flies, midges, no-see-'ems and sand flies all have an unpleasant bite which is best avoided by keeping well covered and by not going out at dusk and dawn, when they are most active. Repellent creams are not very effective and can harm your skin. Antihistamine lotions and pills may help to reduce the itching from insect bites but should not be used to excess.

Stings from insects (such as wasps and bees) or sea creatures (such as jellyfish, weaver fish or anemones) are usually more painful than dangerous, but be alert to multiple stings which have dangerous cumulative effects, stings to the mouth or throat that can swell and block the airway, and stings to people who develop an allergic reaction.

For a sting to the mouth, give the patient ice to suck if at all possible to reduce the swelling and get them to hospital. Multiple stings and allergic reactions manifest themselves in the same way: red blotchy skin, facial swelling and puffiness around the eyes, impaired breathing and a rapid pulse. Get the patient to hospital as rapidly as possible. If the patient remains conscious, help them to find the most comfortable position for breathing freely. If unconscious, put the patient in the recovery position (see pages 138–9).

Bites from venomous snakes are treated by laying the casualty down with the bite at the lowest possible level. Wash the wound as well as you are able and keep the patient as calm and still as possible while help is summoned. Identification of the snake is a help but do not put yourself at risk in order to do so. Never apply a tourniquet, cut the wound or try to suck out the poison.

Blisters

Blisters are there for a reason: the liquid they contain serves to protect and cool the wound. This is the body's way of coping with an injury such as a friction burn and no attempt should be made to drain a blister. Instead, cover the blister with gauze pads and tape or plasters. If the blister has burst by itself do not remove the broken skin, as this will only leave a delicate, unprotected area. Cover the area with plenty of padding.

Useful addresses

Canada
Canadian Yachting Association
1600 James Naismith Drive
Gloucester, Ontario KIB 5N4
Tel   0613 748 5687
Fax   0613 748 5688

France
Federation Francaise de Voile
55 Avenue Kleber
75784 Paris Cedex 16
Tel   01 440 58 100
Fax   01 470 49 012

Germany
Deutscher Segler Verband
Grundgenstrasse 18
22309 Hamburg
Tel   040 632 0090
Fax   040 632 00 928

Ireland
Irish Sailing Association
3 Park Road
Dun Laoghaire
Co. Dublin
Tel   01 280 0239
Fax   01 280 7558

Italy
Federazione Italiana Vela
Viale Brigata Bisagno No. 2
16129 Genova
Tel   010 589 431
Fax   010 592 864

The Netherlands
Koninklidjk Nederlands Watersport
Verbond Postbus 87
3980 CB Bunnik
Runnenburg 12,3981 AZ Bunnik
Tel   0340 570 524
Fax   0340 564 783

New Zealand
New Zealand Yachting Federation
PO Box 90 900
Auckland Mail Centre
Auckland
Tel   09 303 2360
Fax   09 373 5897

South Africa
South African Yacht Racing
Association
PO Box 5036
Cape Town 8000
Tel   021 439 1147
Fax   021 434 0203

UK
Royal Yachting Association
RYA House
Romsey Road
Eastleigh
Hampshire SO50 9YA
Tel   01703 629962
Fax   01703 629924

RYA Scotland
Caledonia House
South Gyle
Edinburgh EH12 9DQ
Tel   0131 317 7388

USA
US Sailing
PO Box 209
Newport
RI 02840
Tel   0401 849 520
Fax   0401 849 520

Glossary

Aback A sail is said to be aback when the wind is blowing against the forward side of it. The *jib* is held aback when the boat is *in irons* or when departing a mooring or the anchor in order to make the *bow* pay off in the right direction.

Abeam In the direction to the side of the boat at 90 degrees to the *heading*.

Aerodynamic force The force generated by the movement of air across a sail or aerofoil. Sometimes referred to as lift.

Aft Towards the back of the boat

Amidships In the middle of the boat.

Apparent wind The wind speed and direction as it is experienced on the moving boat. It differs from the *true wind* as it is affected by changes in boat speed and direction.

Astern 1) Behind the boat. 2) Backwards.

Back 1) To back a sail is to hold it *aback*. 2) An anti-clockwise change of wind direction.

Balance 1) Boat balance – keeping the boat level from side to side. 2) Sail balance – the consideration of the forces acting on different sails.

Batten A wooden or plastic stiffener which supports the *leech* of the sail.

Beam The measurement across a boat at its widest part. Also used to describe a direction in relation to the boat (see *abeam*).

Beam reach A *point of sailing* with the wind coming directly from the side of the boat.

Bear away To turn the boat away from the wind.

Beat To make progress to *windward* by zigzagging *close hauled* on alternate tacks.

Beaufort scale A scale from 0 to 12 which describes the force of the wind.

Bermuda rig A Bermudan-rigged boat has a tall mast and large triangular sails unsupported by a gaff at the top.

Block A pulley to pass a rope through.

Boat trim The way a boat floats related to the fore and aft line.

Bolero Wetsuit jacket.

Boom A *spar* which supports the *foot* of a sail.

Boom groove Groove in the *boom* which the *foot* of a sail feeds into.

Bow The front end of a boat.

Broach The tendency for a boat to round up towards the wind when sailing downwind.

Broad reach A *point of sailing* with the wind coming from diagonally astern.

Buoyancy aid Foam jacket which assists personal flotation.

Burgee A small flag often carrying club insignia, which can be used to indicate wind direction.

Cagoule A waterproof jacket.

Centreboard A wooden or steel swivelling plate which is lowered down through the centreboard case to minimize the sideways drift of a sailing boat.

Chafe The wear of a rope due to rubbing.

Chainplate Strong fitting on the *hull* to which the *shrouds* are attached.

Chart datum The lowest expected level of tide. Used as a reference point on charts.

Cleat A fitting that secures a rope allowing easy release.

Clew The lower furthest *aft* corner of a sail.

Close hauled The *point of sailing* where the boat is sailing as close to the wind as possible.

Close reach See *fine reach*.

Compass course A boat's *heading* described by degrees of a compass.

Course made good The track along which the boat travels after tide and leeway have taken effect. Also described as *ground track*.

Crutch Support for an *oar*, commonly described as a *rowlock*.

Cunningham A control line used to pull down and tighten the front edge of a sail. Sometimes called a *downhaul*.

Daggerboard A board which slots down through the hull and which has much the same effect as a centreboard in reducing the movement of the boat sideways through the water.

Dagger grip The grip usually used to hold the tiller extension on a centre mainsail-rigged dinghy.

Dead run Sailing with the wind exactly behind you.

Displacement The weight of water a boat displaces when floating.

Downhaul See *cunningham*.

Downwind In the direction in which the wind is blowing.

Drying height The vertical height above *chart datum* of a charted object that covers and uncovers with the tide.

Fairlead A fitting that leads a rope in a particular direction and guards it against *chafe*.

Fender An object, usually inflated, that acts as a cushion and protects a boat's hull from another boat, pontoon, wall, etc.

Fine reach A *point of sailing* between *close hauled* and a *beam reach* with the wind about 55–80 degrees off the bow.

Flake To lay out a *warp* or chain so that it will run freely when paid out.

Foot The lower edge of a sail.

Forestay Part of the *rigging* that holds the mast up. Usually made of wire it leads from the top of the mast to the *bow* of the boat.

Forward (pronounced forrard). Towards the front of the boat.

Free wind A wind direction that allows the course to be held with the wind coming from *abeam* or *astern* so you are sailing on a *reach* or a *run*.

Gaff A *spar* that supports the top edge of a (four-sided) gaff sail.

Go about See *tack* 1)

Goose-wing To sail on a *run* with the *jib* and *mainsail* set on different sides of the boat.

Gooseneck The fitting which links the *boom* to the *mast* allowing free swinging from side to side and up and down.

Ground track See *course made good.*

Gunter rig A gunter-rigged boat has a four-sided sail with a short luff. The head of the sail is supported by a near-vertical spar which extends well above the top of the mast. This allows for a shorter mast, so the rig is popular on trailed boats where a shorter mast is easier to handle.

Gunwhale (pronounced gunnel) The upper extremity of the hull or deck edge.

Gybe To turn the stern of the boat through the wind.

Halyard A rope or a wire used for hoisting a sail.

Hank A small clip which is used to attach a sail to the stay.

Head The top corner of a triangular sail, or the top edge of a four-sided sail.

Heading The direction in which a boat is pointing or its *compass course* given in degrees or points of the compass.

Heave to To stop the boat in the water using a balance of forces of the sails and the rudder

Heel 1) The angle at which a boat leans over when sailing.
2) The lower or inboard end of a mast, boom or bowsprit.

Helm The device which works the *rudder* to steer a boat. In small sailing boats usually a *tiller.*

Helmsman The person (male or female) who steers the boat.

Hove to See *heave to.*

Hull The main body of the boat, its sides and bottom.

In irons When a boat is head to wind and temporarily unable to pay off on either *tack.*

Jamming cleat Cleat which secures a line by holding it just between two sets of 'teeth'.

Jib The triangular sail furthest forward on the boat.

Keel The lowest part of the hull which runs its fore and aft length and projects down into the water to reduce *leeway*.

Keel-stepped mast A mast whose heel fits down into the bottom of the boat.

Kicking strap A tackle which controls the shape and twist of the mainsail.

Knots A measure of speed in nautical miles per hour. One knot equals 1.852kph (1.15mph).

Laminar Smooth flow of fluid along a surface. Used to describe efficient flow of air across the sails or water along the keel or centreboard.

Leech The aft edge of a sail.

Leeward (pronounced loo'ard) Downwind or away from where the wind is coming from.

Leeway The tendency for a boat to move diagonally sideways due to wind effect.

Lift See *aerodynamic force*.

Longjohn Long-legged wetsuit trousers which come up to the chest and attach over the shoulders.

Loose footed Where a fore and aft sail is either not set on a *boom* or where the *foot* is not laced or held in a boom groove.

Luff The leading edge of a sail.

Luff up To turn towards the wind.

Lying to Stopping in the water with the sails flapping and the wind blowing across the boat.

Mainsail The principal sail of a sailing boat, set on the mast.

Mainsheet The running rigging which is used to trim the mainsail.

Make fast To secure firmly.

Making way A boat is making way if it is *under way* and moving through the water.

Mast A vertical spar which on a sailing boat has the prime use of carrying the sails.

No go zone The imaginary area which defines the limits of the boat's ability to sail close to the wind.

Oars Usually made of wood, an oar is used as a lever to pull the boat through the water.

Offshore wind Wind blowing from the land out on to the water.

Onshore wind Wind blowing from the water on to the land.

Outhaul Control line used to tension the *foot* of the sail.

Painter The cord or rope attached to the bow of a boat and used for tying it up or being towed.

Peak The top corner of a *gaff sail.*

Pilotage Navigating a vessel in inshore waters.

Plane For a boat to sail quickly and rise up and over its bow wave, skimming its way along the surface.

Point of sailing A series of terms (close hauled, broad reach, etc.) describing the angle between a boat and the wind direction.

Port The left-hand side of the boat (when looking towards the *bow*).

Port tack Sailing with the wind coming from the *port* side of the boat.

Reach A *point of sailing* with the wind coming from the side of the boat. See *fine reach, beam reach* and *broad reach.*

Reef To reduce the size of the sails to allow for strong winds.

Reef pennant A line rigged to pull down the luff or leech of a sail when reefing.

Reeve To pass a rope through a block.

Rigging The collective term for all the wires and ropes that support the spars (standing rigging) and those used for hoisting, lowering and trimming the sails (running rigging).

Rowlock A space cut in the boat's *gunwhale* to take the *oars.* See also *crutch.*

Rudder The blade at the stern of the boat which is moved by the tiller and which steers it.

Run To sail with the wind directly behind you.

RYA Royal Yachting Association.

Sail trim The adjustment of the angle the sail presents to the wind to ensure maximum sailing effectiveness.

Salopettes Chest high trousers.

Shackle A metal fastener with a removable pin mostly used for attaching various parts of the rigging.

Sheet Rope controlling the angle a sail presents to the wind.

Shrouds Part of the rigging holding the mast up, supporting it from either side.

Sounding The measurement of depth on a chart measured from *chart datum* down to the sea bed.

Spar A term which collectively describes masts and booms, etc. on boats.

Starboard The right-hand side of the boat (when looking towards the *bow*).

Starboard tack Sailing with the wind coming from the *starboard* side of the boat.

Stay Rigging that holds the mast in position on the fore-and-aft line. On a dinghy there is usually only a *forestay* but larger boats usually have a *backstay* as well.

Steamer A one-piece wetsuit with long arms and legs.

Step To put the mast into position.

Stern The back of the boat.

Stow To put away.

Swig To take up the final tension when pulling on a halyard. Sometimes referred to as to sweat.

Synoptic chart A weather map showing lines of equal barometric pressure and positions of troughs, fronts and centres of high and low pressure.

Tack 1) To turn the bow of a boat through the wind. 2) The lower forward corner of a sail. See also *port tack* and *starboard tack*.

Telltales Lengths of wool or ribbon used on sails to check for correct *sail trim*.

Throat The upper forward corner of a gaff sail.

Thwart A transverse seat in a boat, hence the term athwartships.

Tiller A bar which is connected to the *rudder*, enabling the steering of the boat.

Tiller extension Another bar used to extend the tiller allowing the *helmsman* to sit out to balance the boat.

Topping lift A rope, usually found on larger touring dinghies, which supports the *boom* when the sail is lowered.

Topsail A sail hoisted above the mainsail on a gaff-rigged boat.

Training run A *point of sailing* between a *broad reach* and a *dead run* where the *jib* just starts to collapse in the lee of the *mainsail*.

Transit An imaginary line marked by the lining up of two fixed objects which is used to assist *pilotage* or the assessment of tidal stream influence.

Transom The flat face at the aft end of a boat's hull.

Trim See *sail trim* or *boat trim*.

True wind The wind speed and direction as it would be experienced if the boat were standing still. See also *apparent wind*.

Under way A boat that is not connected to the sea bed or tied up alongside a pier or pontoon is said to be *under way*. It may not necessarily be moving through the water. See also *making way*.

Upwind In the direction towards the wind.

Veer A clockwise change of wind direction.

Warp Rope used for anchoring or tying up the boat.

Windward Upwind or towards where the wind is coming from.

Index